PERFECT PHRASES™

for
ESL
Conversation Skills

PERFECT PHRASES™

for

ESL

Conversation Skills

Premium Third Edition

Hundreds of Ready-to-Use Phrases That Help You Express Your Thoughts, Ideas, and Feelings in English Conversations of All Types

Diane Engelhardt

New York   Chicago   San Francisco   Athens   London   Madrid
Mexico City   Milan   New Delhi   Singapore   Sydney   Toronto

ISBN   978-1-264-28563-1
MHID   1-264-28563-9

eISBN   978-1-264-28564-8
eMHID   1-264-28564-7

McGraw Hill Language Lab App

Streaming audio recordings that support this book are available via the McGraw Hill Language Lab app, which is available online at www.mhlanguagelab.com and, in mobile form, from the Apple and Google Play app stores.
See inside cover for more details.

Contents

Part 2   Phrases for Discussions

Chapter 7   Opinions   145

Acknowledgments

I would first like to express my gratitude to McGraw-Hill Professional for the opportunity to publish this book, to my first editor, Holly McGuire, for choosing me for this particular project and to my publisher, Christopher Brown, for his support in growing this book.

I would also like to acknowledge the valuable insights my colleague and friend, Barb Donaldson, has provided along the way.

My thanks go out as well to my students: Yuko, Joo-Weoun, Hye-Sin, Chae-Rin, Mayumi, and Satoko for their perceptive feedback.

Last but not least, my appreciation to my husband, Erich, for his support and encouragement.

Introduction

Who Can Benefit from Using This Book?

*P*erfect Phrases for ESL: Conversation Skills was written for ESL students and learners who want to improve their conversation skills inside and outside of the classroom. The content was selected to familiarize you with the kind of language native English speakers use regularly in everyday conversations and discussions at home, school, and work. Although it was written with intermediate-level speakers in mind, there is something for every motivated learner who aims to develop his or her ability to participate in conversations and discussions on a broad variety of topics.

How to Use This Book

The book consists of fourteen chapters divided into four parts: phrases for conversation, discussions, special occasions, and telephone and video conversations. Progressing in depth and difficulty, this third edition covers topics relevant to everyday life.

Objectives

These indicate the skills you can expect to gain from using the phrases in each chapter.

Phrases

Parts 1 to 3

The first three parts cover phrases for everyday conversation.

Each chapter begins with typical conversation openers and contains a collection of topic-related phrases that will guide you through a natural conversation or discussion. Although the phrases are organized thematically, they are not exclusive to any one topic. Where appropriate, reference is made to phrases that appear in previous chapters and come in handy when you discuss different subjects.

Part 4

The four chapters in this section present phrases that are commonly used when you make telephone calls for both personal and business purposes, and these are organized from formal to informal. Because the content of a telephone conversation does not differ greatly from a face-to-face conversation, the ☐ symbol refers you to useful phrases from Parts 1 and 2. You will find these phrases under the given section heading and page number, e.g., Discourse Markers, page 30.

Because language is closely tied to a country's culture and customs, many phrases are organized from formal to informal, indirect to direct, strong to mild, and in degrees of politeness so that you can choose the phrases that are appropriate to use in different situations. The information ⓘ symbol will also alert you to language or culture tips.

You will see that some phrases and parts of phrases appear:

- in **bold** type
- between slashes (/)

Bold type indicates variable phrases that require additional information. For example:

→ **Let me introduce** my fiancée, Alice. (Chapter 2)

→ **Why don't you** try doing volunteer work? (Chapter 3)

Slashes are used to show how a phrase in bold type can be completed with various information. For example:

→ **Don't you look** charming / pretty / handsome today! (Chapter 3)

→ **Please accept my apologies** for the mistake / oversight / inconvenience / trouble. (Chapter 9)

Slashes also indicate how a phrase can be varied with the use of prepositions, gerunds or infinitives, or synonyms. For example:

→ I **plan to** sail / **plan on** sailing around the world some day. (Chapter 6)

→ **What's your view / take / stand / position** on the changes to our curriculum? (Chapter 8)

Phrases that are not indicated in bold type are fixed expressions and can stand on their own. For example:

→ What a pity! (Chapter 5)

→ I couldn't agree with you more! (Chapter 7)

Of course it is not necessary for you to master or even attempt to master all of the phrases under each heading and subheading. One or two may suit your purposes quite nicely. Choose the phrases that fit your personal style, and once you're comfortable using them, you can try out another one. Listen carefully to native English speakers and make a note of the phrases that you hear them use.

Dialogues

The dialogue in each chapter shows you how native English speakers might use the particular phrases in a typical conversation. Consult the McGraw Hill Language Lab app for native-speaker recordings of all fourteen dialogues in the book. If you are learning English in a classroom situation, you can act out the dialogue as a skit or use it as a model for a conversation role-play.

Topics for Practice

At the end of each chapter you will find a list of topics to stimulate conversation. Practice with a friend or classmate. The more people you include in the conversation, the merrier.

Vocabulary Notes

There are blank lined pages at the end of each chapter for you to record new vocabulary. Make a point of writing down the English definition. As you will notice, some words and phrases cannot be easily translated into your native language. Remember: It will be much easier to converse in English if you learn to think and explain yourself in English.

A Final Note

In the end, the best and only way to develop your conversation and discussion skills is to talk. I sincerely hope that *Perfect Phrases for ESL: Conversation Skills* will accompany and guide you on the road to successful communication!

Go for it!

PERFECT PHRASES™

for

ESL

Conversation Skills

PART 1

Phrases for Conversation

"Conversation is the laboratory and workshop of the student."

—Ralph Waldo Emerson

CHAPTER 1

Small Talk

Objectives

- ■ to introduce yourself
- ■ to carry on a basic conversation about yourself and others

Chanwon is waiting for his connecting flight to Seattle. He's come to the United States for a year to study English before he returns to Korea to finish his degree in electronic engineering. He has been on short holidays abroad with his family, but this is the first time that he will be living in an English-speaking environment with an English-speaking family. Of course he's nervous about his ability to communicate in a language he has only studied in school. He'd

like to talk to someone while he's waiting for his plane, but he's not sure how to begin or what to say. What if he uses the wrong word, or no one understands him? And what if someone asks him a question he doesn't know how to answer? If only he had more vocabulary! If only he could speak as naturally as everyone around him!

You could be like Chanwon waiting for your flight at the airport with a long trip ahead of you. You could be having a coffee in a café or a meal in a restaurant, standing somewhere in a line, socializing at a party, or interacting with people you've only just met. Situations in which people strike up a conversation out of curiosity or mutual interest, or just to be sociable, present themselves when you are traveling in a foreign country.

Whether you're meeting someone for the first time or connecting with an old friend or acquaintance, most conversations start out on a personal note. At first you're most likely to talk about:

- where you live or come from;
- what you do for a living;
- what brings you to a particular location.

If the conversation continues, you'll usually move on to everyday subjects with which you're familiar such as:

- personal interests and hobbies;
- the weather;

- your environment (the airport, restaurant, hotel, park, beach, etc.);
- your location (city, country, school, or workplace);
- current happenings such as sports and cultural events or the news.

Although English-speaking people tend to engage easily in conversations with strangers, there are certain topics that may be considered too intimate. Topics that should be avoided are:

- marital status,
- age,
- income,
- religion,
- politics.

Phrases

Openers: Excuse Me . . .

Most often a conversation begins with a simple question, a request for information, or a comment about the weather or surroundings. Depending on the person you're talking to and the situation you're in—is the situation formal or casual, is the person close to your age—there are two approaches you can take.

The *indirect approach* is a polite and unobtrusive way to test the waters in case the other person isn't interested in talking at length:

→ May / could I borrow your newspaper / magazine / the salt and pepper?

→ Could you tell me if this is where the plane leaves for Houston?

→ Would you happen to know a good restaurant / a nice hotel?

→ I was wondering if you're from around here. This is my first visit to London.

→ Sorry to bother you, but is this seat taken / is anyone sitting here?

→ Would you mind telling me where you got that book?

→ Could I trouble / bother you for change? I don't seem to have any quarters.

→ You wouldn't happen to know if there's a café / a bank / a grocery store near here?

The *direct approach* takes the initiative in a friendly, open manner:

→ Excuse me, do you have the time?

→ This is a great hotel, isn't it?

→ I can't believe how busy the airport is today.

→ Nice day, isn't it / eh?

→ So, what brings you here?

→ Do you come here often?

→ Are you from here?

Talking About Yourself

A conversation with a stranger is a good opportunity not only to pass the time but also to practice your English. If the person to whom you are speaking is in the mood to continue the conversation, most likely he or she will be interested in finding out more about you.

→ Nationality	I'm Korean / Japanese / German / Mexican.
→ Residence	I'm from Seoul / Kyoto / Hamburg / Guadalajara.
	I come from Korea / Japan / Germany / Mexico.
→ Age*	I'm twenty-five / thirty-two / in my forties.
→ Marital status**	I'm single / married / divorced / widowed.

---

*ⓘ In English-speaking countries it is not common to talk about your age or to ask a complete stranger his or her age. In fact, it can be considered rude, particularly if the person is much older or much younger than you are.

**ⓘ Again, marital status can be considered personal information, and a person may take offense if asked if he or she is married or not. Some people may not wish to mention if they are divorced or widowed.

→ Job   I'm an engineer / a teacher/
                                 a student / a systems analyst.

                               I'm in advertising / in electronics /
                                 in insurance.

                               I'm self-employed / retired.

                               I'm with McGraw-Hill / AT&T /
                                 Siemens.

→ Hobbies and interests   I'm interested in sports / fashion /
                                 traveling / art.

                               I'm into aerobics / gourmet
                                 cooking / pottery.

Showing Interest

It is important and polite, of course, to show interest in what your conversation partner tells you; otherwise what's the point of talking to someone? While it is courteous to respond to the person you have just met, it is even more important to be sincere and to reply in a comfortable, natural manner.

formal   That must be very exciting / challenging /
              interesting!

          That sounds very interesting, indeed!

          Now, isn't that interesting!

          You don't say / don't mean it!

          You're kidding!

          How interesting!

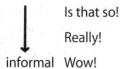

Is that so!

Really!

informal Wow!

Introducing Yourself

If you and the person you've been talking to hit it off, you might want to introduce yourself. Here are some tips when making introductions:

■ In English-speaking cultures, it is usual for people to introduce themselves with their first names rather than their family or surnames. It is very rare that Americans or Canadians will introduce themselves as **Mr**. or **Mrs**. Brown. If they give both their first and last name, for example "I'm Judy Smith", they will usually expect you to call them by their first name. Also in the English language there is no distinction between formal and familiar address, as is the case in many other languages. "You" is "you" regardless of age, social status, or familiarity.

■ Be careful not to confuse "how are you" and "how do you do." **How are you** is a question and requires an answer: **I'm fine, thanks** or **Not too bad** (see Asking about Someone's Well-Being, page 23). **How do you do** looks like a question but is really a greeting, and it is acceptable to respond with **How do you do**, or one of the phrases that follow. If you want to know about someone's health, it's better to ask, **How are you feeling?** or **How are you?**

■ Traditionally people shake hands when they make introductions, particularly in business or formal situations. Men almost always shake hands, whereas women may or may not. When meeting a woman for the first time, wait for her to offer her hand.

■ In more casual and informal situations shaking hands is not always the custom. Young people will use gestures, such as waving their hand, to acknowledge the person. If you are not sure what to do in a particular situation, do as others do.

■ We use the verb **to meet** when we want to say that we make a person's acquaintance. If someone asks you: **How did you meet your husband** or **wife**, they mean *how were you first introduced*, not when did you see him or her last.

Example:
A: How did you meet your husband?
B: Actually he was a friend of my brother's from his college days, and at first I didn't even like him.

formal	**May I introduce myself?** My name's Mary Sutherland.
↕	**Let me introduce myself.** I'm Jun-Hwi Kim.
informal	By the way, **I'm** Jutta Hofmann.

■ Responses

formal	How do you do.
↕	My pleasure.
informal	Nice / pleased to meet you.

Breaking the Ice

Talking to someone you've just met can be awkward, especially if you're not sure what to say or ask. Walking away or cutting the conversation short can appear rude and unfriendly. So what can you talk about to break the ice?

If you feel uncomfortable about asking direct questions, "yes or no" questions show that you're interested in the other person and allow the other person to elaborate if they wish to. Native English speakers are often more direct and will almost always ask strangers where they're from and what they do for a living.

Questions to Ask if the Person Is New to the City

→ Is this your first time to New York?

→ Have you been to Victoria before?

→ Are you new to the company?

→ Are you familiar with this area?

→ How long have you been here?

Questions to Ask Why the Person's Here

→ Are you here on business / a holiday?

→ Did you come here to study English / to travel around?

→ Do you plan to stay here long?

→ Which school / university are you studying at?

→ How long are you staying / visiting?

Questions About the Person's Experiences So Far

→ Have you seen much of the city / country?

→ So how do you like it here so far?

→ How was your flight / trip / first lesson?

→ The weather's been great / nice / very cold, hasn't it?

→ Are you used to / have you gotten used to the food yet?

Questions About the Person's Personal Information

→ Where are you from?

→ Where do you call home?

→ What part of Brazil / Rio de Janeiro do you live in?

→ Are you traveling alone or with family / friends?

→ Do you like music / theater / sports / skiing / swimming?

→ What do you do for a living?

→ What kind of business are you in?

If you're the person being introduced, you'll want to show interest in the other person as well. If your answer to a question is negative, it's a good idea to respond with a question so as not to cut off the other person or force him or her to carry the conversation.

→ Have you been here long? **No, I've just arrived. And you?**

→ Have you been to the museum? **No, not yet. Have you?**

→ Are you staying very long? **No, only a few days. How long are you here for?**

So as not to sound like a parrot, you can respond to a question by asking the same thing in another way:

→ Where are you from? **From Osaka. And where do you call home?**

→ Are you here on business? **Yes, I am. What / how about you?**

→ How long are you staying here? **Two weeks. Are you here very long?**

→ What do you do for a living? **I'm an architect. And where do you work?**

Other acceptable topics for small talk are the weather, local sights and attractions, the event you are attending, and the services or facilities in the hotel where you're staying.

Staying in Touch

→ It's been great seeing you / talking to you.

→ We'll have to stay in touch.

→ We should get together again / sometime / soon.

→ Look me up next time you're in town.

→ Don't forget to give me a call / send me an e-mail.

→ Drop in sometime.

Responses

→ Give me a call / a ring / a buzz.

→ That's a deal.

→ I'll do that.

→ I'll sure try.

→ You can count on it!

→ For sure.

→ You bet!

Saying Good-Bye

formal It was a pleasure meeting you / talking to you.

Nice / great to have met you.

I'm glad we met.

I enjoyed our conversation / talking to you.

I hope we meet again soon.

I look forward to working with you.

Maybe we'll see each other around.

Till tomorrow / next time.

Good-bye.

Bye / bye now / bye-bye.

See you around / later / then.

See you.

So long.

informal Too-da-loo / ta-ta / cheerio.

Responses

formal | The pleasure was all mine.

My pleasure.

Same here.

Likewise.

Ditto.

Me, too.

I hope so.

informal | Sure thing.

Wishing Someone Well

→ Have a nice day / a pleasant evening / a safe trip / an enjoyable flight back.

→ Enjoy your flight / stay / tour.

→ Good luck to you!

→ All the best.

→ Take care now.

→ Take it easy.

Responses

→ You have a nice day, too.

→ I wish you the same.

→ Same to you.

→ Likewise.

→ You, too.

Dialogue: Small World

This dialogue takes place at an airport café. Underline or highlight the phrases from the chapter.

Jenny: Excuse me. Do you have the time?

Brett: Uh, sure. Let me take a look. It's ten to.

Jenny: Thanks. I'm sorry to bother you, but my watch seems to have stopped.

Brett: No problem.

Jenny: I'm always a little nervous about the time when I have to fly somewhere.

Brett: I understand. You wouldn't want to miss your flight.

Jenny: No, that's for sure. I'm flying to Las Vegas to see a friend and I'm really excited.

Brett: Yeah, Vegas is quite the place.

Jenny: Have you been there before?

Brett: Actually, I live there.

Jenny: You're kidding! Have you lived there long?

Brett: About five and a half years now.

Jenny: Wow, then you must know the city pretty well.

Brett: Well, I'm away on business a lot, but I get around.

Jenny: I'm kind of the opposite.

Brett: And where do you call home?

Jenny: I work in Vancouver, but I'm originally from Salt Spring Island. I bet you've never heard of it.

Brett: As a matter of fact, I was there on a sailing trip last summer.

Jenny: Really? That's interesting.

Brett: It's a beautiful place.

Jenny: One of the best. Wow, this *is* a small world!

Brett: So how long are you staying in Vegas?

Jenny: Just a week. Unfortunately, that's all the time I could get off from work.

Brett: Look, here's my card with my cell phone number and e-mail. By the way, my name's Brett.

Jenny: I'm Jenny.

Brett: Nice to meet you, Jenny.

Jenny: Nice to meet you, too.

Brett: I'll be back in three days. Maybe we can get together for a night out.

Jenny: That's a deal. Hey, I'd better get going.

Brett: Yeah, you don't want to miss that plane.

Jenny: It was great talking to you, Brett.

Brett: Same here.

Jenny: And thanks for your card.

Brett: My pleasure. Have a good flight, and don't gamble away your money.

Jenny: I won't. Bye-bye.

Brett: See ya!

Topics for Practice

What can you say about:

1. your job or studies;
2. your family;
3. the city / town or country you come from;
4. the city / town or country you're visiting;
5. the flight or journey you've been on;
6. the reason you're at your location (hotel, airport, restaurant, city, school);
7. the weather or climate;
8. something you've seen or done on your trip;
9. a recent sports, social, or cultural event;
10. a very different custom or habit that you've noticed?

Vocabulary Notes

_____

_____

_____

_____

_____

_____

_____

_____

_____

_____

_____

_____

_____

_____

_____

_____

_____

_____

_____

_____

CHAPTER 2

Past Experiences

Objectives

- to introduce family members, friends, and acquaintances
- to talk and inquire about past experiences and events

Jutta is showing her husband, Franz, around the city of Victoria, British Columbia, while they are visiting on a holiday. Three years ago when she was offered an exciting new job as an editorial assistant with a publisher of trade journals in Nuremberg, Germany, Jutta attended an intermediate English course at a language school in Victoria to brush up on her high school English. During her three-month studies she met many foreign students and made friends from Japan, Korea, and Mexico.

Although Jutta has lost touch with Yuko, Ryeowon, and Patricia, she often wonders what happened to them, and how their lives have changed. While Jutta and Franz are visiting the Butchart Gardens, she spots a group of Korean tourists. Their guide looks so much like Ryeowon, but that would be too much of a coincidence! The group moves closer, and Jutta calls Ryeowon's name. The young woman turns around with a look of surprise on her face.

f you have traveled or studied abroad, chances are that when you least expect it you will run into someone—a former classmate or colleague, a teacher, or a friend of a friend—on a holiday, at a conference, at a wedding, or even on the street. Time has passed, and, of course, you have a lot to catch up on. There are so many experiences you have to share, so many stories you'd like to tell, and so many questions you're anxious to ask.

Phrases

Openers: Greetings

formal	Good morning / day / afternoon / evening!
	Hello!
	Hi!
	Hi there!
	Hi ya!
	Howdy!
informal	Hey!

(**i**) We say **Good night** instead of **Good-bye** when we part company late in the evening or before we go to bed.

The expression **Hey** was once considered rude, but it has now become a common greeting among family members and young people who know each other well.

Greeting Friends and Acquaintances

When you haven't seen someone for a long time, it's customary to begin the conversation by asking about the other person's well-being and by commenting positively on changes that you may notice.

formal

Hello, Isaak! Remember me?

Say, Paolo. I don't believe it! Is that really you?

Hi! Aren't you So-Hee?

What a pleasant surprise!

Fancy meeting you here.

Hey, long time no see.

Speak of the devil.

Hi there!

informal   Hey!

Addressing Someone Whose Name You Can't Remember

➜ **I don't mean to be forward, but** don't I know you from somewhere?

➜ **Could it be that** we've met before?

→ You remind me of someone. **You wouldn't happen to be** Margarete?

→ **Don't I know you from** last year's book fair in Frankfurt?

→ Haven't we met before?

→ You look **familiar**.

Asking About Someone's Well-Being

→ How are you?

→ How are things?

→ How have you been?

→ How's it / everything going?

→ So, how's life been treating you?

→ How've you been getting along / making out?

Responses

(i) It has become common to say **How do you do?** or **How are you doing?** as a greeting, in which case it's not necessary to give an answer.

→ Just fine. And you?

→ Great. And yourself?

→ Couldn't be better. How about you?

→ Pretty good.

→ Can't complain.

→ Not too bad.

General Comments

→ It's good / great / to see you again / to run into you like this.

→ You're looking great / good / well.

→ You haven't changed much / at all.

→ You've hardly changed.

→ It's been ages / so long / such a long time.

→ I can't believe it's you.

→ Is that really you?

→ Small world, isn't it?

Making Introductions

Whether you're traveling on business or for pleasure, you are most likely in the company of another person. When you introduce friends and family, you should choose familiar language (see Chapter 1), and introduce the person with his or her first name.

When introducing a third person, it is a good idea to give some information about the person:

■ how the person is related to you: husband/wife, fiancée/ fiancé, son/daughter, niece/nephew, etc.

■ where the friend or acquaintance is from and what's his or her job

formal

I would like you to meet my coworker, Steve.

Let me introduce my fiancée, Alice.

This is my husband, Bob. Bob, this is Carol.

↓
informal

Steve, **this is** Sergei.

Hey, Masa. Meet Jorge. We're old friends from school.

Responses

formal

↑
↕
↓

informal

My pleasure to make your acquaintance, Steve.

How do you do, Alice.

Nice to meet you, Bob. Carol's told me a lot about you.

Masa, **how's it going**?

Catching Up

Once you've gotten reacquainted, you will want to find out about friends and acquaintances that you have in common and reminisce about "the good old times."

Asking About Recent Events

→ What have you been doing with yourself all this time?

→ Where've you been hiding / keeping yourself?

→ What's cooking / up / new / the scoop?

→ What have you been up to?

→ So, what's the story?

→ Anything new?

Asking About Friends and Acquaintances

→ I wonder what ever happened to / became of Guido.

→ Have you heard anything from Tomoko?

➜ Have you seen Maria-Teresa lately?

➜ Do you know anything about our teacher?

➜ Did you know that Andre got married / promoted?

Talking About Friends and Acquaintances

➜ The last I heard, Guido had changed jobs.

➜ It's hard to keep up with Anastasia. She's always on the go.

➜ I haven't heard from her for ages.

➜ We used to e-mail, but lately we seem to have lost touch.

➜ That's great news. I'm really glad / happy for him.

Shared Experiences

➜ Remember when we held a mock election in our afternoon class?

➜ Didn't we have fun / a good time on that camping trip?

➜ Wasn't the food in the cafeteria delicious / awful?

➜ Don't you miss the beach / scenery / going out to the disco?

➜ Those were the good old days / good old times!

Past Experiences

Reconnecting with old friends or acquaintances is an opportunity to exchange stories about your experiences. Time has passed since you last saw each other, and you are interested in finding out what has happened in the meantime.

■ Asking About Past Experiences

→ What have you been doing with yourself all this time?

→ Have you been up to anything exciting / interesting?

→ What happened after you went back to Japan?

→ I'm dying / anxious to hear about your new job / what you've been doing.

→ So, what have you been up to?

→ So, fill me in.

■ Introducing an Experience

→ You'll never guess what happened to me in Phoenix.

→ The most interesting thing happened to me the other day.

→ Let me tell you about what happened while I was in Toronto.

→ Know / guess what happened?

→ Guess what?

Transitions and Connectors

Everyone has a story to tell. Whether it's a joke or short anecdote; a lengthy account of an adventure, game, or event; a report of an accident or mishap; or the summary of an intriguing conversation, these accounts make up a large part of your daily conversations. To tell a good story you don't have to be a professional entertainer; you just need to connect your thoughts and to add a little drama at the right moment.

Asking About Experiences

→ **What happened** on your vacation / trip / when you went to France?

→ **How did you make out** while you were in London?

→ **So how did your visit** to New York **go / turn out / work out**?

→ **Whatever became of** your plans to take part in the Tour de France?

→ **What did you experience** on your cruise to Alaska?

→ **Did anything interesting / unusual / exciting happen** to you on your holiday?

→ **I've always wondered / wanted to ask you about** your year in California.

→ **We'd love to hear** the latest news.

Beginnings

→ **One morning / afternoon / day** on our holiday in France we decided to go for a short walk in the countryside.

→ **To start / to begin with / first off / it all started when** we had breakfast and got ready for our walk.

Sequence

→ **Next / the next thing,** we followed a set of red and white trail markers from our hotel to the Lot river.

→ **Along the way** we saw a sign pointing to a historical village on a hill overlooking the river.

→ **Then / so then** we climbed up and spent some time checking out the village.

→ **In the meantime** it had started to rain, **so** we went into some shops.

→ **While** we were looking around, the rain stopped and we continued on our walk.

→ **On the way** we passed through another small village.

→ We kept on walking but **after a while** we noticed that there were no more red and white trail markers.

→ **A few miles / kilometers later** we asked for directions at a farmhouse, but the woman said she didn't know of any trail leading back to our hotel.

→ **After that / afterward** we decided to turn around and go back to the village.

Adding Drama and Information

→ **All of a sudden / suddenly** it started to rain again, **only this time** it started raining cats and dogs.

→ **By the time** we got to the village we were wet, hungry, and tired.

→ **To top it off / to make matters worse,** when we got to the village café, they had finished serving lunch, and all we could have was a cup of coffee.

→ **Unfortunately** that day was a national holiday, and there was no bus service.

→ **In fact / as a matter of fact** there was no taxi in the area, either.

→ **Luckily / fortunately / as luck would have it,** the rain soon stopped and we continued on.

→ **Lucky for us** we came to a sign pointing to the village where our hotel was located.

→ **However,** it was seven kilometers away and **before we knew it,** it was already late afternoon.

→ **Frankly / actually / truthfully / to tell you the truth** we thought we were never going to find our way back before dark.

→ **As it turned out** we came to the river where at last we saw the red and white trail markers.

Concluding

→ **Finally** we made our way along the muddy riverbank.

→ **In the end** we got back to our hotel **just before dark** and **in time for** dinner.

→ **To make a long story short / long story short** we cleaned up, had dinner, and went to bed!

→ **The moral / lesson of the story is** when you go on a walk in a foreign country, never leave your hotel without a map.

→ **It just goes to show you that** you should never leave your hotel without a map.

Discourse Markers

Because people think on their feet when they hold a conversation, they use "little words" called *discourse markers* to fill in the gaps when they are searching for words. Discourse markers do not change the meaning of the sentence. In fact they have no literal meaning and can become a bad habit, as in the case of "like" or "you know," when the speaker uses them too often. Common discourse markers in English include the following.

Starters

→ As you know / you see / see

→ Now / then / okay / all right

→ I mean / well / so / oh

→ Say / why

Examples:

Well, I'd love to hear about your trip.

Now, what have you been up to?

So, after we got to the airport, we had to wait five hours.

Fillers

→ Uh / er / em

→ Like / you know

Examples:

We stayed at this great hotel, **you know**, right on the beach.

It was, **like**, the best place we ever stayed.

Question Tails and Tags

(i) Whereas many languages have fixed question tags, such as *n'est-ce pas* in French, *verdad* in Spanish, and *nicht wahr* or *gell* in German, for instance, English uses the same helping verbs that form a question, and each question tag depends on the verb tense. Common examples are: **It's a nice day, isn't it?** or **You haven't met my fiancée, have you?** For help with question tags, you can consult a good grammar book.

➜ Know what I mean?

➜ Don't you think?

➜ Or not?

➜ Right?

➜ Eh?*

Examples:

Traveling is one of the best ways to gain experience, **don't you think?**

Terrific game, **eh?**

Enjoyment and Pleasure

formal   I really enjoyed myself on my vacation / at Disney World.

We had a great / good / nice / grand / splendid / super time.

Everyone had a lot of fun.

It was the best time I've ever had.

The trip was really worthwhile / worth it.

I'll never forget it.

---

*ⓘ *Eh* is considered a typically Canadian question tail, but it is also used in Great Britain and former British colonies, although the pronunciation will vary slightly.

We got a lot out of it.

I really got a kick / bang out of it.

informal   It was a ball / a gas / a blast!

Expressing Emotions

Emotions can be difficult to express, particularly in a language that is not your native tongue. To say how you feel and to make sure that others understand your feelings, you will need to use specific phrases and idiomatic expressions.

Astonishment and Surprise

→ That's incredible / fantastic / amazing / far out / unreal / awesome.

→ That's hard / difficult to imagine.

→ I don't believe that for a minute!

→ You've gotta be kidding / joking!

→ You're putting me on / pulling my leg.

→ What a coincidence!

→ No way!

Belief

→ I believe you / it.

→ I can imagine.

→ That's true / for sure.

→ Isn't that the truth!

→ I bet!

Ending the Conversation

➔   We'll have to get together / do this again sometime soon.

➔   It was great to see you again.

➔   I'm so glad we ran into each other.

➔   I really enjoyed seeing you again.

➔   Let's keep in touch / get together again.

➔   Take care / take it easy.

➔   Catch you later / another time.

Time Expressions

ⓘ   When referring to the time in English-speaking countries, native English speakers generally differentiate between night and day by using a.m. and p.m. For example, breakfast time is at 7:00 a.m. and dinnertime is at 7:00 p.m. (rather than at 19:00). It is also common to say **seven in the morning** or **evening** in order to clarify the time of day. Rather than ten to twelve or a quarter after twelve, native English speakers shorten it to **ten to** or **quarter after**.

➔   Time: **at** 5:00

➔   Day: **on** Monday / Friday

➔   Month: **in** June

➔   Year: **in** 2005

→ Date: **on** the 2nd of March / March the 2nd

→ Deadline: **by** 7:30 / tomorrow / Saturday / the end of the month

→ Other: **in** the morning / afternoon / evening

at night / the beginning / the end

on the weekend

from 9:00 **to** / **until** 12:00

since 8:00 / Friday / January / 1995 / last week / I got here

for two hours / three days / six months / ten years / a long time / many years

during lunch / the flight / my holiday / the week

Dialogue: Long Time No See

This dialogue takes place at a golf club. Underline or highlight the phrases from the chapter.

Susan: Mark, I don't believe it. There's someone I know over there. Linda!

Linda: Oh, my gosh. Susan. Susan Macrae, is that you?

Susan: Susan Edison now, but yeah, it's me.

Linda: No way! Nice to see you, Susan. Like, it's been ages!

Susan: I know. Gee, you haven't changed a bit.

Linda: I don't know about that. What have you been doing all this time?

Susan: Oh, the usual. You know, life, work, family. And yourself?

Linda: Well, that's a long story.

Susan: I'd love to hear it, but first let me introduce my husband. Mark, meet Linda Franzen. Or at least it was.

Linda: Still is. Hi, Mark. Nice to meet you.

Mark: How do you do, Linda.

Susan: Linda and I lived in the same dorm at college.

Mark: So this is *the* Linda . . . ?

Linda: I hope you haven't told any stories.

Susan: Nothing that isn't true.

Linda: Now I'm really in trouble! Anyway, how come I haven't seen you two here before?

Mark: Well, we only joined the golf club this summer.

Susan: Mark got transferred to Portland last summer, and since then we've been busy getting settled into our new house and then there are the kids and all their activities.

Linda: You always were a go-getter, Susan. Are you still into acting?

Mark: Acting? Is there something I should know?

Susan: Oh, it was just amateur stuff. But that wasn't all we did for kicks, was it?

Linda: Don't remind me.

Susan: The good old college days, huh? But didn't you go to Europe for a while?

Linda: Yeah, I traveled around and then I ended up living in Italy for ten years.

Susan: Wow! What were you doing in Italy?

Linda: Well, first I had a ball just touring around and then I got a job teaching English. That's how I met Giorgio. You'll have to meet him. Look, let's get together for dinner.

Susan: We'd love to. There must be a million things to catch up on. Like whatever happened to Brenda.

Linda: You'll never guess, but she ended up in New Zealand.

Susan: What do you know! We used to have a riot together!

Linda: Didn't we! Anyway, sorry I have to run, but give me a ring. I'm in the book.

Susan: So are we. Edison on Cormorant Drive.

Linda: Got it! Well, it was great meeting you, Mark.

Mark: Same here.

Linda: Susan always had good taste. Hope to see you soon.

Susan: You can count on it!

Topics for Practice

Tell a story about:

1. your last holiday;
2. your last business trip;
3. one of the happiest moments in your life;
4. the luckiest or funniest thing that's ever happened to you;
5. an unforgettable travel experience;
6. an accomplishment at work or school;
7. the history of your company / town or city;
8. a disaster or accident that you have experienced;
9. how you met your best friend / wife / husband / girlfriend / boyfriend;
10. how you got your job.

Vocabulary Notes

_____

_____

_____

_____

_____

_____

_____

_____

_____

_____

_____

_____

_____

_____

_____

_____

_____

_____

CHAPTER 3

Likes, Dislikes, and Interests

Objectives

- ■ to express likes, dislikes, and preferences
- ■ to talk and ask about hobbies, interests, and leisure time activities

Miho and Lanxin are two of the many international students who attend high school in North America every year. Not only will they have to get used to a new school system and English-only instruction, but they will find themselves in a new cultural environment without their families and the friends they have grown up with. Although both girls know that going to high school in the

United States or Canada is a great opportunity, they are unsure of how well they will fit in and how easily they will be able to make friends. What will they have in common with their classmates? How similar will their interests be? Will they be included in the activities, sports, and games that interest American and Canadian teenagers? And what if their classmates ask them questions they don't know how to answer?

Common likes and interests are the basis on which you make friends and develop lasting relationships. They are also the subjects you probably talk about the most frequently.

Phrases

Openers: Feeling Things Out

➜ Do you have any hobbies?

➜ Are you interested in sports / music / computers?

➜ Do you have a favorite kind of food / music / sport?

➜ How do you spend your spare / free / leisure time?

➜ What do you do / like to do in your spare / free / leisure time?

Likes

I like vs. *I'd like*

→ *I like ice cream* means that ice cream gives me pleasure or enjoyment; in other words, it tastes good to me.

→ *I'd like (would like) ice cream* means that I don't have any ice cream at the moment, but I wish I had some.

Examples:

I'd like a big bowl of ice cream right now, wouldn't you?

I'd really like to see the Grand Canyon some day.

Also, we use *I'd like* to request or order something, or to offer something to someone.

Examples:

I'd like a coffee to go, please.

I'd like two tickets to the 8:00 show.

Would you like a soda or a glass of juice?

Verbs

stronger

Jane **loves / adores** music / going to live concerts.

I **can't get enough of** this sunshine.

I **fancy** gourmet food / cooking for friends.

Silvio **enjoys** tennis / working out at the gym.

We **like** historical films / cross-country skiing.

less strong

Nouns

stronger

Glen has **a passion for** orchids / gardening.

You're **an** animal **lover / lover of** animals.

I'm **an admirer / a big fan of** Martin Scorsese.

less strong

Verbs / Adjectives with Prepositions

stronger

I'm **crazy / mad / wild / thrilled about** San Francisco / sightseeing.

Suzette's **passionate about** children / teaching.

Aron's **big on** football / working out at the gym.

I'm **fond of / keen on / partial to** mystery novels / rollerblading.

less strong

Impersonal Subjects

stronger

Community work is Abdul's **passion**.

Stefan's job is **everything to** him.

The sunset last night was **awesome**.

How does a trip to the Greek islands **tickle your fancy**?

Luigi's is **my kind of** restaurant.

Modern design **appeals to** me.

less strong

Feelings for People

stronger

I **love** / **adore** you.

My children **mean a lot** / **the world** to me.

Tom **thinks the world of** Marie.

Sarah's **crazy** / **mad** / **nuts** / **gaga about** Sean.

You **send** me.

I **care a lot** / **very much for** my grandparents.

I **like** / **really like** my new roommate **a lot**.

less strong

Slang Expressions

➜ I'm **really** / **heavily into** modern art / painting.

➜ Sun-Woo **gets off on** football / playing tennis.

➜ Claudia **really digs** your new outfit / John Mayer.

➜ This CD **really turns me on**.

➜ Hiking is **right up my alley**.

➜ That leather jacket is **hot** / **so hot** / **totally hot**.

➜ Alfonso's a **really cool** / **neat** guy.

Rejoinders

➜ I like pizza. **So do I** / **I do, too**.

➜ Satoko's crazy about sushi. **Me, too**.

➜ Kate couldn't live without her dishwasher. **Same here**.

➜ Andrea really gets off on reggae. **Same goes for me**.

➜ This music's hot. **You bet!**

Dislikes

The simplest way to express a dislike is to make a positive into a negative. Many of the previous expressions can be made into clear dislikes.

Examples:

I **like** dancing, but I **don't like** square dancing.

You're **fond of** comedies, but you're **not fond of** romantic comedies.

Sascha's **really into** jazz, but his sister isn't **into** music at all.

Choosing the right phrase to express your likes and dislikes is always an individual matter. It is also a matter of how deeply or strongly we like or dislike something or someone.

Verbs

stronger

I **hate / can't stand / can't stomach** greasy food / waiting in long lines.

My sister **detests** snakes / getting up early.

Mami **can't put up with** cigarette smoke / other people smoking.

Jürgen **minds** the rainy weather / taking the bus.

Noura **dislikes** housework / going shopping on Saturday.

We **could live without** winter / having to shovel snow.

less strong

Adjectives + Prepositions

stronger

↑

I'm **sick of / tired of / sick and tired of** sandwiches / doing the dishes.

Pierre's **fed up with** his old car / working overtime.

We're **averse to** crowded places / taking the subway.

Rinaldo's **not fussy about** airports / flying.

↓

less strong

Impersonal Subject

stronger

↑

The traffic in this city **makes me sick**.

Politicians **get on my nerves**.

Barking dogs **bug / annoy** me.

Milan's cooking **doesn't do it / doesn't cut it / doesn't do anything for me**.

Plastic furniture is **not my taste**.

Abstract art **leaves me cold**.

The service here isn't **anything to write home about**.

Living in a basement suite is **not my cup of tea**.

↓

less strong

Feelings for People

stronger

↑

Camille **hates / can't stand / detests** gossips.

I **don't want anything to do with** Marco.

The Smiths **won't have anything to do with** the Joneses.

↓

less strong

Slang

stronger

↑

This movie **sucks / sucks big time!**

Getting stuck in traffic really **stinks**!

Our last test was **the pits**!

This painting is **god-awful**!

The traffic **drives me crazy / up the wall / around the bend**.

Loud people **really turn me off**.

Working on Saturdays isn't **my first choice**.

François's **not into** sports/jogging.

I **don't get off on** football / watching sad movies.

That idea is **totally out there / off the wall**.

↓

less strong

Rejoinders

As you can see from Chapter 1 and the previous examples, you can agree with a positive statement by adding "too"; for example: **I do, too**, or **Me, too**. When you agree with a negative statement, use **either** or **neither** instead. A simple rule to remember is:

- **too** for two or more positives;

   Examples:

   I really love an espresso after a meal. **I do, too**.

   We get off on jazz. **Me, too**.

- **either** or **neither** for two or more negatives.

   Examples:

   I can't stand this rain. **I can't, either**.

   I don't care much for junk food. **Neither do I / I don't, either**.

Asking About Likes and Dislikes

→ **How / how much do you like** rap music / my new camera / playing video games?

→ **What's your favorite** color / music / game?

→ What kind of sports / movies / food **do** you **prefer / favor**?

→ What / which fashions / TV shows **are** you **into**?

→ **What do you think of** tennis / the weather / Beyoncé's new song?

Preferences

stronger

We**'d rather / much rather / sooner** read **than** watch television.

I **prefer** coffee **to** tea / walking **to** biking.

A compact car would be / is **my preference over** a sedan.

Buying a house is **preferable to** renting an apartment.

Most foreign language students **favor** English **over** other languages.

I **tend to** avoid crowded places / studying at night / reading nonfiction.

I'd **choose** going to the beach **over** sightseeing in the city.

My first choice would be to pay cash.

I'll **take** summer **over** winter **any day**.

I'd **go for** eating out **instead of** cooking.

Blue is **my favorite** color.

less strong

Interests

Personal Subject

→ I'm **interested in** tennis / video games / painting / cooking.

→ Chia **finds** yoga / traveling **fascinating** / **interesting** / **stimulating**.

→ Norbert's **involved in** local politics / recycling / helping kids with cancer.

→ Lourdes **helps out** / **volunteers** at the library / at the SPCA / at the hospital.

→ Tomo's **a member of** a conversation club / the Red Cross / the YMCA.

→ Yi-Ting **belongs to** a book club / Amnesty International / Greenpeace.

Impersonal Subject

→ Tennis / painting / cooking **interests** me.

→ Documentary movies are **of great interest** to me.

→ Modern art **intrigues** / **fascinates** me.

Common Interests

→ We **have** a lot **in common**.

→ We **share** the same interests.

→ We're both **interested** in the same things.

→ Europeans and Americans **share common ground** in their values.

Desires and Dependency

Sometimes your feelings toward something or someone go beyond simple likes or preferences to become desires and dependencies. Although in some cases you may be expressing your true feelings, in others you may exaggerate for the sake of effect.

Desires

stronger

↑

I'm **dying for** a cup of coffee.

I've got **a craving for** a hot fudge sundae.

I **could really go for** a day at the beach.

Yoko **longs / yearns** to see her family in Japan.

Our class **feels like** a party / having a party.

We're **in the mood for** a trip to the mountains / taking a trip.

Amani **wants** to learn Spanish.

Sanjay**'d like / love** to live overseas for a couple of years.

↓

less strong

Dependency

stronger

↑

Sam **couldn't live / exist / get along / make it without** his cell phone.

I'd **die without** my car / my iPad.

Carlo's **addicted to** chocolate / hockey / shopping / jogging.

Julie's **stuck on** tennis.

Min-Jung **can't think about anything but** fashion.

We **don't know what we'd do without** our car.

Pavel really **depends on / relies on** his laptop.

less strong

Indifference

→ We **kind of / sort of like** this painting.

→ I **don't mind** our new office.

→ The performance was **rather interesting**.

→ The movie was **not bad / so-so**.

→ The weather **doesn't matter** to me.

→ **It makes no difference to me** if we go out or stay home.

→ **It's all the same to me** if it snows or rains.

→ I can take it or leave it.

→ It's six of one and half a dozen of the other.

Making Offers

Choice of words and tone applies to situations in which you offer something to someone. When you are dealing with strangers or customers, **would like** is more polite than **want**.

If you want to refuse an offer from someone, a simple answer is always best. It is not necessary to explain yourself or to give a detailed reason that may sound insincere or offend the person who is making the offer.

Offers

formal	**Would you like** a cup of coffee?
	May I / Can I get / offer you something to read?
	Would / do you care for another drink?
	Shall I call you a taxi?
	Is there anything I can get / bring / offer you?
	Will there be anything else?
	How about if I pick you up at 8:00?
	How about another dance?
	Have another cookie, **why don't you?**
	Want more pie?
informal	**Cigarette?**

Positive Responses

→ *Would you like a cup of coffee?*

formal	Yes, please. That would be nice / fine / lovely / great.
	That's nice of you to offer.
	I'd love one. Thank you.
	Yes, I'd appreciate that.
	That's kind of you to offer.
	Sure thing!
informal	Why not!

Negative Responses

→ *Can I get you something to drink?*

formal   No, thank you. I'm fine for now.

Thanks, but I'd rather not.

I've had enough / my share, thank you.

No, I don't drink / don't need anything.

I'll pass, but thanks.

I'm good, thanks.

Maybe later.

informal Not now / at the moment.

Dates and Invitations

When you meet someone you like and get along with, it's only natural to want to see him or her again. You can invite someone to your home for dinner, to a club for a game of golf, or to attend a social occasion such as a wedding, birthday party, or celebration.

(i) A date, on the other hand, is usually an arrangement between two people who have a romantic interest in each other, although it is also common for friends to make a lunch or theater date, for example. Traditionally it has always been the man who asks the woman for a date and who pays the check, but it is now acceptable, though not usual, for a woman to ask a man out or for them to split the cost.

Dates

formal   **I'd like to ask you out to** dinner / a movie / the game on Friday.

Would you like to go out on a date / with me to a movie?

Do you fancy going out with me on a date?

Care to go out with me for a drink?

informal   **How about** going out together sometime?

Invitations

formal   **We'd like to invite you to** our grand opening.

Would you like / care to join us for a drink after work?

I was wondering if you'd care to attend our luncheon.

Do you feel like a game of golf?

How about going to dinner on Friday?

informal   **Want to** hang out at the mall after class?

Positive Responses

formal   I'd be happy / more than happy to come / to join you.

That'd be nice / fine / good / great.

That sounds nice / good / great / like fun.

Of course. I'll look forward to it.

Thank you. We'll be there.

We'd love to.

I wouldn't want to miss it.

Sounds great / good.

informal   Sure, why not!

Negative Responses

formal   **I'd like / love to, but unfortunately** I've got other commitments / plans.

I appreciate the invitation, but I've made other plans.

Thanks for the invitation, but I have other plans.

I'm sorry, but I won't be able to.

That's nice of you, but I'm afraid I can't.

Sorry, we're **not into** golf.

Parties are **not our thing**.

informal   I'll pass, **but thanks anyway**.

Another Time

formal   Why don't we save it for another time / later.

Can we make that another time?

How about a rain check?

informal   Maybe another time / later.

Offering to pay

→ Let me get that.

→ Lunch is on me.

→ My treat.

→ It's on the house.*

Expressing Emotions

Excitement

→ I'm looking forward to the reunion / seeing my classmates.

→ I can't wait to start school / can hardly wait to start school.

→ I'm really excited / thrilled / stoked / fired up / wound up about the game / going to the game.

→ I'm raring to go / chomping at the bit.

→ I'm all gung ho.

Enthusiasm

→ Hurrah / hurray / hooray!

→ Good move / good show!

→ Far out / cool / sweet / brilliant / excellent!

→ Wow / yippee / yeah!

---

*This phrase is used when the owner of a restaurant or bar gives a guest something for free.

Compliments

→ **I'd like to compliment you on** the delicious meal / on the great party.

→ Bright colors really **suit / become you**.

→ **You look great / fantastic** in that dress / shirt.

→ Those earrings **look good on you / go well with** your hair.

→ **I really like** your T-shirt.

→ **Don't you look** charming / pretty / handsome today!

Responses

→ I appreciate the compliment.

→ That's nice of you to notice / to say that.

→ Thanks for the compliment.

→ Really? Do you think so?

→ Why, thanks!

Dialogue: What's for Dinner?

Underline or highlight the phrases from the chapter.

Mike: Hey Sarah, what's for dinner?

Sarah: Gee, I've been so wound up about my job interview tomorrow that I haven't given dinner a single thought.

Mike: I could really go for something spicy like chili.

Sarah: Spicy? I'm not into spicy food right now, and actually I don't feel much like cooking.

Mike: Well, don't look at me. I hate cooking. And besides you're the expert. That spaghetti you made the other night was awesome.

Sarah: Flattery will get you nowhere. What do you say to ordering a pizza?

Mike: Good idea. I'm crazy about pizza. In fact, my favorite is Hawaiian.

Sarah: I can't stand pineapple on pizza.

Mike: I didn't realize you were so fussy.

Sarah: I'm not. It's just that I prefer to eat fruit for dessert, not with the main course.

Mike: How about if I order Hawaiian and you order something else?

Sarah: But a whole pizza is too much, and I don't care for leftover pizza.

Mike: Well, there's always Chinese food. Don't we have a menu somewhere?

Sarah: The last time we ordered from that place the food was greasy and it took them forever to deliver. But you know what? There's a new Greek restaurant downtown. It'll be my treat.

Mike: But doesn't Greek food have lots of garlic? Just the thought of garlic turns me off.

Sarah: Garlic's good for you. I can't get enough of it myself.

Mike: At this rate we'll never get anything to eat. I'm starving.

Sarah: Can't you think about anything but your stomach?

Mike: Not when it's getting close to dinnertime.

(The phone rings and Sarah answers.)

Ally: Hi, Sarah. Sorry for the late notice, but would you and Mike care to come over for dinner tonight?

Sarah: Yeah, sure. Is there anything I can bring, like a salad?

Ally: No, just bring yourselves. Is six-thirty all right?

Sarah: That's fine. See you then. Mike, guess what? Ally's invited us over for dinner.

Mike: Sweet! Did she say what she was having?

Sarah: Really, Mike! Hey, we should pick up some wine on the way. What do you think, red or white?

Mike: Actually, I'd rather get some beer.

Sarah: Oh no, here we go again.

Topics for Practice

How much do you like . . .

1. walking in the rain;

2. music;

3. getting up early;

4. spending the day at the beach;

5. horror movies;

6. the colors red or blue;

7. violence on television;

8. Mozart;

9. apple pie and ice cream;

10. going to parties;

11. traveling to foreign countries;
12. going to the dentist;
13. gambling;
14. Christmas;
15. cats or dogs;
16. your boss or teacher;
17. video games;
18. snowboarding;
19. shopping;
20. team sports?

Vocabulary Notes

_____

_____

_____

_____

_____

_____

_____

_____

_____

_____

_____

_____

_____

_____

_____

_____

_____

_____

_____

_____

CHAPTER 4

Objects and Processes

Objectives

- ■ to describe objects, products, and processes
- ■ to compare and evaluate objects, products, and processes

Andrea has been promoted to senior buyer for a well-established company that sells footwear and leather accessories primarily in Italy. Recently the company has taken over a chain of shoe retailers with outlets in Austria, Switzerland, and Germany. In his new position Andrea will be traveling frequently to Asia to discuss the products with the company's suppliers. As well, he will be attending international shoe fairs where he will be buying new products.

Although Andrea is familiar with the technical terms of the shoe fashion industry, he will now have to discuss his company's products in more detail. When it comes to dealing with foreign suppliers, he needs to ask and answer questions in a precise manner so that he will avoid mistakes and misunderstandings that could cost his company time and money.

On a daily basis many of your conversations focus on objects, devices, and machines that you use, produce, buy, and sell at work, school, home, or the store. In addition to describing objects and processes, you need to explain how to use or operate devices and machines and to give others instructions and explanations.

Phrases

Openers: Take a Look!

→ How'd you like to see / take a look at my new iPad?

→ I've got this tool I'd like to show you.

→ How about I show you my flat-screen TV?

→ Want to see what I've got?

→ Take a look at what I just bought.

→ Check this out!

Describing Objects

Talking about objects, machines, and processes can be a complicated business. For this purpose you may require specialized language and vocabulary (engineering, IT, telecommunications, medicine, manufacturing, food preparation, etc.). Since you're probably already familiar with the technical terms, all you need are some simple and useful expressions that you can readily employ.

➔ What's this for?

➔ What's it called?

➔ What have you got there?

➔ What's this supposed to be / to do?

➔ What kind of machine / object / tool / device / gadget is it?

➔ What's the make / brand name / model / serial number?

ⓘ If English speakers don't know the particular name of an object or device, they use nondescript words, such as: **device** / **gadget** / **widget** / **contraption** / or slang expressions, such as: **doodad** / **dooie** / **doohickey** / **thingamabob** / **thingamajig** / **whatchamacallit**.

Examples:

What am I supposed to do with this **doodad** on the top?

The Dollar Store sells all kinds of **gadgets** and **contraptions**.

Please hand me that **thingamabob** over there.

Measurements and Dimensions

→ What size is it?

→ How big is it?

→ How long / wide / high / deep / big around is it / does it measure?

→ What's the length / height / depth / circumference?

→ How much does it weigh / carry / hold?

→ What's the maximum load / capacity?

→ It's 10 inches / 22.5 centimetres **long / wide / high / deep / around**.

→ **The length / width / height / depth / circumference** is 10 inches / 22.5 centimetres.

→ It **measures** 10 inches / 22.5 centimetres **in length / width / height / depth / circumference**.

→ It's a **5-metre-long** vehicle **/ a ½-inch-wide** band **/ an 80-foot-high** building **/ a 20-ounce** bottle.

→ It **weighs** 10 pounds / 4.5 kilograms.

→ It's 10 pounds / 4.5 kilograms **heavy**.

→ It's **the size of** a baseball / a book / a giant sail.

→ It **fits** into your pocket / glove compartment / closet.

→ It's 10 **by** 5 **by** 2 inches / 22.5 **by** 12.5 **by** 5 centimetres.

→ It's **flat / two-dimensional / three-dimensional**.

→ It **holds** 1 gallon / 4 litres.

Shape

→ What does it look like?

→ What shape is it?

→ It's the shape of a cigar / balloon / walnut.

→ It's cigar-shaped / balloon-shaped / walnut-shaped.

→ It looks like / resembles a balloon in shape / size.

Common Geometrical Shapes

→ Circle / circular

→ Cone / conical

→ Cube / cubic

→ Cylinder / cylindrical

→ Hexagon / hexagonal

→ Octagon / octagonal

→ Oval

→ Rectangle / rectangular

→ Semicircle / semicircular

→ Sphere / spherical

➜ Square

➜ Triangle / triangular

➜ Tube / tubular

Properties and Features

Describing the size and shape of an object with standard phrases is relatively easy. Discussing an object in more detail, however, requires a wider variety of phrases.

Material

➜ What's it made of?

➜ What materials did they use to make it?

➜ It's **made / constructed of** glass / plastic / wood / metal / leather.

→ It **consists of** glass / plastic / wood / metal / leather.

→ It's a steel rod / a gold ring / a stone wall / a brick house.

Color

→ What color is it?

→ What color / colors does it come in?

→ It's white / red / blue / yellow and beige.

→ It's dark / medium / light / pale / bright green.

→ It's a yellowish / reddish color.

Origin

→ It was made / produced / manufactured / assembled in China / the USA / Germany.

→ It is / was made / produced / manufactured by Sony / Philips.

→ It was designed / built / constructed by an architect.

→ The telephone was invented by Alexander Graham Bell.

Method of Production

→ It was made by hand / machine.

→ It's handmade / machine-made / man-made / mass-produced.

→ It was prefabricated / pre-assembled / extruded / molded / mixed / packaged / wrapped.

→ It was made to order / custom-made.

Properties

→ It's waterproof / ovenproof / fireproof / childproof.

→ It's heat resistant / water-resistant / stain resistant.

→ It's dishwasher safe.

→ It's dense / solid / liquid / gaseous.

Features and Functions

→ What can it do?

→ What functions / features does it have?

→ It comes in four colors / ten sizes / six patterns.

→ It's multipurpose.

→ It operates / runs on electricity / battery / solar power / fuel cells.

→ It's easy to use / cheap to operate / efficient to run.

→ It performs efficiently / in all weather conditions.

→ It has all the frills / bells and whistles.

Quality

high ↑

It's good / high / top / superior / excellent / premium quality.

It's high-tech / state-of-the art / up-to-the-minute / advanced technology.

It's the newest / the latest / most sophisticated of its kind on the market.

It's top of the line / a leading brand.

It's high performance.

It's government approved / Consumer Reports rated / safety tested.

It's mediocre / so-so / average / overrated.

low   It's poor / inferior / substandard quality.

Cost and Estimates

→ How much is it?

→ How much does it come to?

→ How much do you pay / what do they charge?

→ What's the price?

→ What's the daily rate?

→ What's the damage?

American and Canadian Currency*

→	**$1.29**	one dollar and twenty-nine cents / a dollar twenty-nine
→	**$15.99**	fifteen dollars and ninety-nine cents / fifteen ninety-nine
→	**$5.00**	five dollars / bucks
→	**25 cents**	a quarter
→	**10 cents**	a dime

---

*ⓘ Australia and New Zealand also use the dollar but have different coins.

➜ **5 cents**   a nickel

➜ **1 cent**   penny

➜ It was / cost $50.

➜ They charged me $50.

➜ The price was $50.

➜ It's / was worth $50.

➜ It's valued / appraised at $50.

➜ It came to $50.

expensive   It's priceless / valuable.

It cost me an arm and a leg.

It was reasonable / affordable.

It was on sale / reduced / half-price.

I bought it at a discount.

It was 25 percent / a third off.

It was a real deal / bargain / steal / dirt cheap.

I got it for next to nothing.

cheap   It was free / complimentary / a giveaway.

If you paid more for something than it was worth, you can say:

➜ I paid through the nose.

➜ They ripped me off.

➜ It was a real rip-off.

When you don't know the exact cost or value of an object, you will have to come up with an estimate or approximate value.

→ It's worth **about / around / approximately / circa / nearly** $1,000.

→ It's **in the neighborhood / in the region of** $1,000.

→ It's $1,000 **give or take / plus or minus / more or less**.

→ **A ball-park figure** is $1,000.

→ It has **an estimated / approximate value of** $1,000.

→ An **estimate / guesstimate** would be $1,000.

→ We **estimate** its value at around $1,000.

Use and Availability

Purpose and Use

→ What does this do?

→ What's this used for?

→ How can I use / operate / utilize this?

→ What's its purpose / use / function?

→ How does it work / go / operate?

→ It's for cutting material / hammering nails / storing data.

→ A refrigerator is used for keeping food cold / to keep food cold.

→ This product is designed to save time.

→ It serves / acts as a water heater / an answering machine / a calculator.

→ It has a bunch of useless gimmicks.

Availability

→ Where / how did you get / buy it?

→ Where's it sold?

→ Where is it available?

→ Who / which store carries it?

→ It's sold at Walmart / Best Buy / Home Depot.

→ You can get / buy / order it online.

→ Future Shop carries it.

Popularity

→ Espresso machines are really "in."

→ An iPhone is the latest thing / fashion / rage.

→ X is the leading brand.

→ Everybody's buying it.

→ You've got to have it.

→ It's in high demand.

→ The stores can't keep it in stock / on the shelves.

Making Comparisons

There are many ways to compare objects, processes, and functions. Note that the comparisons are shown in the following order: adjective, count noun, non-count noun, verb, and adverb.

Expressing a Difference with a Positive Verb

→ A is **unlike / different from / different than / distinct from / dissimilar to** B.

→ A **differs from** B.

→ A is **better /** bigg**er /** cheap**er /** eas**ier to use /** hand**ier** to carry **than** B.

→ A is **more** advanced / expensive / efficient / innovative **than** B.

→ B is **less** advanced / expensive / efficient / innovative **than** A.

→ A has **more** features / functions / uses / advantages **than** B.

→ B has **fewer** features / functions / uses / advantages **than** B.

→ A has **more** capacity / power / storage space / value **than** B.

→ B has **less** capacity / power / storage space / value **than** A.

→ A costs / weighs / sells / is worth **more than** B.

→ B costs / weighs / sells / is worth **less than** A.

→ A smells **better /** runs fast**er /** operates **more** efficiently **than** B.

→ B smells **worse /** runs slow**er /** operates **less** efficiently **than** A.

Expressing a Difference with a Negative Verb

→ B is not **as** big / durable / useful / efficient **as** A.

→ B doesn't have **as many** features / functions / uses / advantages **as** A.

→ B doesn't have **as much** capacity / power / storage / value **as** A.

→ B doesn't cost / weigh / sell **as much as** A.

Expressing Similarity

➜ A is **like / similar to / equal to / comparable to / the same as / much the same as** B.

➜ A and B are **alike**.

➜ A functions / acts / works **in the same way as** B.

➜ A is **as** big / good / easy to use / advanced / expensive **as** B.

➜ A has **as many** features / functions / uses / advantages **as** B.

➜ A has **as much** capacity / power / storage space / value **as** B.

➜ A costs / weighs / sells / is worth **as much as** B.

To emphasize the lack of difference, we can add adverbs such as **just, exactly,** or **precisely**.

Examples:

This coffee is **just as tasty** as the leading brand.

A has **exactly as many built-in functions as** B.

Expressing a Small Difference

➜ A **is almost as / nearly as / isn't quite as** / big / good / easy to use / advanced / expensive **as** B.

➜ A **has almost as many / nearly as many / doesn't have quite as many** features / functions / uses / advantages **as** B.

➜ A **has almost as much / nearly as much / doesn't have quite as much** capacity / power / storage space **as** B.

➜ A **costs almost as much as / nearly as much as / doesn't cost quite as much as** B.

Expressing a Large Difference

→ A isn't **nearly as big** / good / easy to use / advanced / expensive **as** B.

→ A is **a lot / way / much / far** bigger / better / easier to use / more advanced **than** B.

→ A has **a lot more / many more / way more** features / functions / uses **than** B.

Superlatives

→ C is **the best** / **the worst** / bigg**est** / **the** eas**iest** to use / **the** hand**iest** to carry.

→ C is **the most** advanced / expensive / efficient / innovative.

→ D is **the least** advanced / expensive / efficient / innovative.

→ C has **the fewest** features / functions / uses / advantages.

→ C has **the least** capacity / power / storage space / value.

→ C costs / weighs / sells / is worth **the least**.

Adverbs

For emphasis you can add qualifying adverbs such as: **considerably, definitely, really, by far**.

Examples:

Running shoes A are **considerably cheaper than** Running shoes B.

Printer A is **definitely more compact than** Printer B.

Camera A takes **by far the best** quality pictures.

Machine A is **really the fastest**.

Making Contrasts

To compare and show a contrast, you can use various connectors:

Co-coordinating conjunctions: **but, yet**;

Adverbs: **nevertheless, nonetheless, however, regardless**;

Subordinate conjunctions: **whereas, while, although, even though, though**;

Prepositions: **despite, in spite of, unlike**;

Phrases: **on the one hand, on the other hand, in contrast, at the same time, for all that**.

→ Printer A has many useful functions, **but / yet** it takes up a lot of space.

→ Printer A has many useful functions; **however / nevertheless / nonetheless / regardless** it takes up a lot of space.

→ **Whereas / while** Printer A has many useful functions, it takes up a lot of space.

→ **Although / even though** Printer A has many useful functions, it takes up a lot of space.

→ **Despite / in spite of** its size, Printer A has many useful functions.

→ **Unlike** other printers in its price range, Printer A takes up a lot of space.

→ **On the one hand** Printer A has many useful functions; **on the other** it takes up a lot of space.

→ Printer A has many useful functions. **At the same time** it takes up a lot of space.

Evaluations and Judgments

Praise

→ Camera A is **a good bargain / a good deal / good value for your money**.

→ Camera A **lives up to its name / promise / advertising / reputation**.

→ I've had only **good experiences with** Camera A.

→ Camera A is **worth the money / buying / having**.

→ There's **nothing like** Camera A.

→ You **can't beat** Camera A.

→ Camera A is **beyond comparison**.

→ Camera A is **the best money can buy**.

→ Lotion B **works wonders**.

→ I **couldn't live / do / manage without** my laptop.

Criticism

→ This toaster is a **real piece of junk / garbage / trash**.

→ My DVD player is a **lemon / complete waste of money**.

→ This gadget serves **no useful purpose**.

→ Any product of Company A's **the last thing I'd buy / want**.

→ I've had **nothing but trouble with** this scanner.

→ My battery charger **doesn't work worth a darn / damn / hoot**.

→ These cheap knives **belong in the trash** / **dump**.

→ You can have it!

→ It's like **throwing your money out the window**.

Giving Instructions

The easiest way to describe a process is to refer to the operating manual, user's guide, manufacturer's instructions or, in the case of food preparation, the recipe. Written instructions, however, may not always be at hand, and even if they are, sometimes guides are written in language that isn't easy to decipher. When instructions and diagrams are confusing or ambiguous, you may be asked to assist someone or to explain the process in more detail.

To describe a process or to give instructions, you can do two things:

■ Use command forms such as **press, select, turn the machine on**, etc.

Example:

Press ENTER to start a new line.

■ Use modal verbs such as **have to**, **need to**, or **to be supposed to**.

Example:

You **have to / need to / are supposed to** press ENTER to start a new line.

As you go along, you will have to correct or confirm what the person is doing, and if there's danger of creating a bigger problem, a word of caution might be necessary.

Questions

→ What do I do first / next / then / after that?

→ What am I doing wrong?

→ Why doesn't this work?

→ How come this doesn't work / nothing happens?

→ I can't figure this out / understand this.

→ I can't seem to get this to work.

→ This doesn't seem to work.

The following example shows phrases that you can use to give instructions on how to record a voicemail greeting.

How to Begin

→ **Firstly / first of all / to start off** / tap the Greeting button.

→ **The first / initial step / thing** is to tap the Greeting button.

What to Do Next

→ **The next step / thing** is to tap Custom.

→ **After / following that** tap Record and dictate your greeting.

→ **Then** tap Record and dictate your greeting.

→ **Next** tap Record and dictate your greeting. **When** you've finished recording, tap Stop and review by pressing Play.

How to Finish

→ **Finally / lastly / at the end** tap Save.

→ **The final step / thing** is to tap Save.

Making Corrections

When you give someone instructions, it is sometimes necessary to correct a mistake or give a warning. It is also important to let the person know when he or she is doing the right thing.

→ You have to back up a step / to go back to the first / last step.

→ Go back and start again / over.

→ Give it one more / another try / go.

→ Erase / delete / cancel that and try again / start over.

→ Let's try it another time.

→ You seem to be doing something wrong.

Caution

→ Wait / hold it a second before you go on.

→ Slow down and take it easy / take your time.

→ Make / be sure to press SELECT first.

→ Be careful to adjust the setting / not to press down too hard on the foot feed.

→ Take care to turn the knob gently.

→ Remember / don't forget to press OK.

Confirmation

→ Good, now go onto the next / following step.

→ That's right / correct / the way to go!

→ That's it / the way to do it!

→ Now you're cooking with gas!

→ Now you're on to it.

→ You've got it!

Expressing Emotions

Confusion

→ I can't figure these instructions out for the life of me.

→ I don't know if / whether I'm coming or going.

→ I can't make heads or tails of this.

→ I'm completely / totally lost / at sea.

→ This is over my head / beyond me.

→ This has got me confounded / bamboozled.

Frustration

→ This is driving me crazy / up the wall / around the bend.

→ I'm at my wit's end / at the end of my rope.

→ I don't have a clue / the faintest idea what to do.

→ I can't figure out how to get this to work.

→ I just can't get a handle on this.

→ This has really got me stumped / stymied.

→ I've had it up to here.

→ I'm fed up / sick and tired.

Wonder

→ I'm impressed with the quality.

→ I'm amazed / astonished / flabbergasted / blown away.

→ The sound quality blows me away / boggles my mind!

→ The design knocks my socks off!

→ Wonders will never cease.

→ Holy cow / smokes!

Dialogue: The New Smartphone

Underline or highlight the phrases from the chapter.

Sean: Hey, Paul, check this out!

Paul: What've you got now?

Sean: Get a load of my new Mango smartphone.

Paul: Wow! Is that *the* Mango 3000z? Man, everybody's talking about it. That must have cost you an arm and a leg.

Sean: Well, it wasn't exactly cheap, but it's worth every penny.

Paul: I suppose it has all the bells and whistles.

Sean: Besides all the regular cell-phone features, this baby's got assisted GPS, plus WiFi and mobile broadband access that's much faster than other phones. And I can send and receive e-mails, plus edit messages.

Paul: How many applications can you run?

Sean: Besides the standard built-in apps that come with it, there are literally thousands more to download. And whereas most phones can only do one thing at a time, with the Mango you can run third-party apps and multi-task at the same time.

Paul: I'm impressed big time! By comparison my mobile looks like it came out of the Stone Ages.

Sean: Take a look at the smudge-resistant interface. All you have to do is touch an application like this and there it is!

Paul: The sleek design's pretty cool, too.

Sean: Yeah, and it's light as a feather. It weighs less than five ounces, and is about a fourth of an inch thick so it's definitely pocket-size. And look at this feature. If you want to type a message, it has a QWERTY* keyboard so you don't have to fiddle around with numbers like you do on a normal cell phone.

Paul: Since when are you into typing messages?

Sean: I text all the time, but of course I don't have to now 'cause—and this will knock your socks off, buddy—now I can make video calls right from my Mango.

Paul: How can you do that?

---

*ⓘ QWERTY keyboard: Standard U.S. keyboards have the letters QWERTY arranged on the top left row of keys, giving it its name.

Sean: See, it has two cameras. One on the front here and the other on the back. So what you do is go into your contacts list and find a number. Then you touch video call and bingo. It's easy as pie.

Paul: Get out of here! You're sure it's not just some gimmick?

Sean: No way, man. Mango really lives up to its name. And get this, I can record my own videos and edit them into movies right here on my phone. YouTube, here I come.

Paul: So how are you going to do that?

Sean: Well, I haven't figured it out yet.

Paul: Looks like this smartphone's smarter than you are.

Sean: Says the guy with the fossil phone.

Topics for Practice

Describe the following:

1. a surround-sound system;
2. a microwave oven;
3. an MP3 player;
4. a camera;
5. a sailboat;
6. a dishwasher;
7. a car;
8. a blender or kitchen machine;
9. a pair of running shoes;
10. your dream house or apartment.

Describe how to:

1. send an e-mail;
2. change a car tire;
3. tie a necktie;
4. make coffee;
5. parallel park a car;
6. use an ATM machine;
7. make a pizza;
8. record a movie or television show;
9. download images from a digital camera;
10. burn a CD.

Compare the following:

1. a minivan and an SUV;
2. a laptop and a desktop computer;
3. a walking shoe and a hiking boot;
4. a bicycle and a motorcycle;
5. a house and an apartment;
6. a paperback and an e-book;
7. a television and a radio;
8. a screwdriver and a hammer;
9. an apple and an orange;
10. wine and beer.

Vocabulary Notes

_____

_____

_____

_____

_____

_____

_____

_____

_____

_____

_____

_____

_____

_____

_____

_____

_____

_____

CHAPTER 5

Problems and Advice

Objectives

- to explain a problem and to give advice
- to express sympathy and understanding

Patricia is getting married this summer, and she and her fiancé, Matthew, will be living in San Francisco. Patricia's future in-laws have welcomed her into their family, yet to Patricia they seem quite reserved in comparison to her family in Mexico, who are given to expressing their feelings and opinions loudly and openly. Her English is very good—or so everyone tells her—and she has worked hard to lose her Spanish accent, but she wishes the right words would come to her more naturally.

What will she do if there are problems or misunderstandings that she will have to handle on her own? And how can she bring up a concern without hurting someone's feelings? Will she be able to help if someone asks her for advice or needs a shoulder to cry on? Being there for others is something she is used to in her culture, and she hopes that she will be able to do the same for her future family and friends.

Problems can range from the inconvenience of a machine that won't work; to complaints about the weather, work, or school; to difficulties in our relationships with family, friends, or coworkers; to serious physical, emotional, or psychological conditions. While some people are habitual complainers, others find it difficult to open up and air their grievances. In any case the best way to solve a problem is to talk about it, and in order to get advice, you must know how to make yourself understood.

Phrases

Openers: What's Wrong?

➜ You don't seem to be yourself. Is anything wrong / the matter?

➜ Is there anything you'd like to tell me / talk about?

➜ What seems to be wrong / the matter / the trouble?

➜ What's bothering / troubling / eating you?

→ What's wrong / the matter / the problem?

→ What's on your mind?

→ What's the story with you?

→ Why so glum / down in the mouth?

→ Anything bothering / troubling you?

Stating a Problem

A popular saying advises that when life hands you a lemon, you should make lemonade. In other words, every problem has a solution, and you should try to make the best of things. Nevertheless, problems come in a variety of shapes and sizes, and before you can arrive at a solution, you have to open up.

(i) Native English speakers sometimes ask **"What's your problem?"** when they object to what someone is doing, for example, when someone is looking at them or is angry or upset for no apparent reason. It's not really a question.

Personal Problems

→ I haven't been feeling well / like myself lately.

→ I've been feeling down / blue / out of sorts / out of it / under the weather.

→ I'm just not myself these days.

→ I'm just not up to things.

→ I'm on edge.

Stress

→ I've been feeling really **stressed out / under pressure** lately.

→ I'm **up to my neck / my ears / my eyeballs** in work.

→ I **can't handle / take / deal with all** this pressure anymore.

→ I'm feeling **overworked / overtaxed / overwhelmed / burned out**.

→ The wedding plans **are all getting to be too much**.

→ I **can't seem to manage / handle / deal with / cope with** things anymore.

→ I'm **having a bad / hard time** with my assignments.

→ This new program is **causing me a lot of trouble / nothing but** headaches.

→ I'm **not getting anywhere with** my computer course.

→ I need some **downtime / personal time**.

Problems with Things

→ The remote control **doesn't work / won't work / doesn't seem to work**.

→ I **can't figure out** this answering machine.

→ I **can't get** this switch **to work / to do anything**.

→ The microwave **is on the fritz / kaput / a piece of trash**.

→ My laptop **just bit the dust** / My laptop **had the biscuit**.

Money Matters

→ I'm a little hard up / short on finances / short of money / out of cash at the moment.

→ I'm having trouble making ends meet.

→ I'm broke.

Complaining About a Problem

→ **I'm really bothered / annoyed / irritated about** the construction in the building.

→ I have **a lot on my plate** right now.

→ I'm **having a hard / rough time with** my studies.

→ I'm **not having any luck / success with** my investments.

→ Our new work schedule is **a real nuisance / bother / pain in the neck**.

→ My biology class is **a killer / is killing me**.

→ The traffic is **getting on my nerves**.

→ Getting an extension on my visa is **one big hassle**.

→ I need to **get something off my chest**.

Asking for Help or Advice

Although you may not always want to admit it, sometimes you need to ask for help.

indirect **Do you think you could** help me out / give me a hand with my speech?

I'd like to hear your advice on how to save for my retirement.

What do you think I should do about my visa?

I've got this problem with my car.

I wish I knew how to fix this mess.

Can / could you take a look at my essay?

direct I need some help / some advice.

Asking for Confidentiality

→ I hope you'll keep quiet about this / keep it to yourself.

→ Please don't breathe / say a word to anyone.

→ This is just between you and me.

→ Don't tell a soul.

Response

→ I promise not to tell a soul / to breathe a word.

→ My lips are sealed.

→ You can trust me.

→ You can confide in me.

→ Mum's the word.*

---

*① A British slang expression meaning "don't say a word" or "keep your lips sealed."

Identifying the Cause of a Problem

Asking About the Cause

→ How long has this been going on / happening?

→ When / how did this start / happen?

→ What happened / set things off?

→ What's behind / at the bottom of this?

→ How did this all come about?

→ What's the story?

→ What / who caused the problem / was the cause?

→ Whose fault / responsibility was it?

Blame and Responsibility

→ It's all because of a misunderstanding.

→ It happened by accident / all of a sudden / without warning.

→ It was an accident / a mishap / unintentional.

→ It's all my / your fault / mistake / error.

→ I'm responsible / guilty / the guilty party / the culprit / to blame.

→ I take full / complete responsibility.

→ I blew it / my chance!

→ I take the rap.

→ I screwed up.

→ Blame it on me.

Sympathy and Understanding

When a friend or acquaintance needs a shoulder to cry on, you should show consideration and understanding.

Offering Sympathy

formal

I understand / sympathize completely / totally.

I can imagine what you're going through.

I know exactly how you feel / what you mean / what it's like.

You have my sympathies.

I feel for you.

I'm sorry to hear that.

What a pity / shame!

How awful / terrible / horrible / unfortunate!

That's too bad!

You poor thing!

informal

Asking for Sympathy

→ Try to see / look at things from my side / end / point of view.

→ If only you knew how I feel.

→ Put yourself in my shoes.

→ You have no idea.

Advice and Assistance

Solutions to problems come in the form of suggestions, advice, and offers of assistance. A suggestion leaves it up to the person to accept or reject your advice. In other words, you don't want to be forward or step on anyone's toes. What the person does with the suggestion is up to him or her. Advice, on the other hand, deals more directly with a problem by offering a specific opinion or solution.

Making Suggestions

Problem: Johanna's classmate, Chiao-Jung, is homesick and misses her family in Taiwan.

indirect

May I suggest doing volunteer work to get out and meet people?

I'd like to suggest / recommend doing volunteer work / that you do volunteer work.

Have you ever thought of / considered doing volunteer work?

Has it ever occurred to you to do volunteer work?

Maybe / perhaps you could try doing volunteer work.

You might want to try doing volunteer work.

What you need is to do some volunteer work.

Why don't you do volunteer work?

You could try doing volunteer work.

How about doing volunteer work?

direct **Let's** do volunteer work.

(i) The verbs *to suggest* and *to recommend* require the use of the *subjunctive* and can be tricky to use. The subjunctive looks like the *indicative* (simple present) and is recognizable only when you use the verb *to be*, the third person singular, or the negative.

Example:

I suggest / recommend that you **be** on time / that he **get** more exercise / that they **not worry**.

The easiest way to get around the subjunctive is to use a gerund.

Example:

I suggest / recommend **being** on time / **getting** more exercise / **not worrying**.

Positive Responses

→ That just might be the answer.

→ That makes sense.

→ I never thought of that!

→ It never occurred to me!

→ I'll give it a try!

→ Why didn't I think of that!

→ Now you're talking!

→ Good / great idea!

→ Sounds good to me!

Negative Responses

→ That sounds like too much trouble / hassle.

→ It's useless / pointless / senseless / no use.

→ Thanks, but I don't think that's for me.

→ That makes no sense.

→ What good would that do?

→ A lot of good that does!

→ I'd rather not.

→ You can't be serious!

→ Are you kidding / joking?

→ No way!

Offering Advice

Problem: Moon-Hee's roommate, Salman, is always complaining about never having enough money.

indirect **Don't you think it might be wise / smart / good** to make a budget?

It'd / might be a good idea to make a budget.

The best thing to do would be to make a budget.

It looks to me like you might need to make a budget.

If I were you, I'd make a budget.

The way I see it, you need to make a budget.

You have to / need to / ought to / should make a budget.

All you have to do is make a budget.

I tell you what: make a budget.

direct **You'd better** make a budget.

Positive Responses

➔ Thanks for the advice.

➔ I'll give it a try / do that.

➔ That's the best idea I've heard.

Negative Responses

➔ I know you mean well / your intentions are good, but . . .

➔ That's easy for you to say.

➔ That's easier said than done.

➔ If only it were so easy.

Offering Assistance

Problem: An elderly customer at the café where Meiko works seems to have lost something.

formal How can / may I help you / be of assistance?

Is there anything I can do to help / help you with?

What can I do for you?

Can I give you a hand?

Here, let me help.

informal Need a hand / some help?

Positive Responses

→ That's very kind / thoughtful / considerate / helpful of you.

→ I really appreciate it.

→ That'd be great.

Negative Responses

→ Thanks, but I'll be fine / all right.

→ I can manage / do it myself.

→ Thanks, but no thanks.

Confirming a Suggestion

→ Is that okay / all right with you?

→ Are you okay / all right with that?*

→ How does that work for you?

Positive Responses

→ That's okay / all right / fine with me.

→ That works for me.

→ Perfect.

---

*Saying "Are you okay / all right" means that you are asking about someone's health.

Warnings

Problem: Henrik is planning to travel down the West Coast, but he doesn't have a lot of money so he asks Jose if he thinks it would be okay to hitchhike.

➔ I wouldn't if I were you!

➔ **Be careful / beware of / aware of** dangerous people.

➔ **Don't** hitchhike at night, **or you might be sorry**.

➔ Hitchhiking alone **could get you into trouble**.

➔ **You'd better not** take rides from strangers / strange people.

➔ **Just a heads-up**: hitchhiking can be dangerous.

Last Resorts

If you ask ten people for help with a problem, you will probably get ten different solutions, but there is no guarantee that any of them will work. If you really don't know what to do, a last resort or extreme measure may be your only option.

Problem: Although Ulla has tried different diets, she still can't take off the last five pounds she wants to lose before her wedding.

➔ **If the worse / the worst comes to the worst / if push comes to shove**, you can try fasting.

➔ **If nothing else works**, you can go on a fast.

➔ **Your only other alternative is** to go on a fast.

➔ **If all else fails**, you can go on a fast.

➔ **As a last resort**, you can go on a fast.

➔ **All that's left** is to try fasting.

Appreciation and Gratitude

formal

I'd like to express my appreciation / gratitude for your help.

I really appreciate it / that / your advice.

I'd like to thank you for the good advice / your assistance.

Thank you very much for your assistance / for assisting me.

That's **very kind / helpful / considerate / good of** you.

Your help **means a lot to me**.

I'm most grateful.

Thanks a lot!

You've been a big / great help!

Much appreciated!

I owe you one!

informal   You're a lifesaver.

Responding to a Thank-You

formal	I'm glad I could be of service / of help / of assistance.
	You're welcome / most welcome.
	It's nothing at all.
	It's no bother really.
	Don't mention it.
	My pleasure!
	Not at all.
	Any time.
informal	No problem.

Making Someone Aware of a Problem

There are times when you might have the unpleasant task of making another person aware of a problem. In case you meet with hostility, or the person feels that he or she is being blamed for something that is not his or her fault, you will have to approach the subject in a manner that will not offend the person. Depending upon the gravity of the situation, you can choose between an indirect and a direct approach.

Problem: Maria gets along well with her colleagues, but they share a very small office, and their new colleague, Tiffany, is not very good at putting things back where they belong.

indirect ↑

I hate to say this / to tell you this, but I think we should have a little talk.

I wish there was another / easier way to put this, but we need to talk.

There's something I've been meaning to bring up.

Don't be offended / get me wrong, but I have to make you aware of something.

It's come to my attention that you haven't been putting things back.

I don't know how to say this, but everything in the office has its place.

Could I have a word with you about something?

Maybe you should think about putting things back in their place.

We have a situation / problem on our hands.

It's time to sit down and have a heart-to-heart.

direct ↓

We need to talk / do something / make some changes.

Complaints

Problem: Sascha is trying to study, but he can hear loud music coming from his neighbor's apartment.

indirect   **I hate to bother / trouble you, but** do you think
            you could turn down the music?

            I'm sorry to say this, but your music is bothering me.

            Do / would you mind turning down the music?

            Do you think you could turn down the music?

            Excuse me, but could you turn down the music?

            Would you please turn down the music?

            How about turning down the music?

            Please turn down the music.

            Turn down the music, **will you**?

direct   Turn it down!

Responses

➔ Sorry, I didn't realize that / I didn't know / I wasn't aware.

➔ I'm sorry, it won't happen again.

➔ I didn't mean to bother you.

➔ Really? That's too bad.

➔ No problem / trouble at all.

Reassurances

If someone's been through a rough patch or has even lost a loved one, you can reassure him or her that everything will be all right or offer comfort or condolences.

Making Reassurances

→ Everything's going to be / to turn out all right.

→ Everything will work out, just you wait and see.

→ Things have a way of working themselves out.

→ Believe me, it's going to be okay / fine.

→ It's not as bad / half as bad as it seems.

→ You'll be fine / okay / right as rain.

→ You're doing the best you can.

→ We can get to the bottom of this.

Calming Someone Down

→ There's nothing to worry / fret / get upset about.

→ Don't worry / fret / freak out / sweat it.

→ Don't lose any sleep over it.

→ Don't take it to heart / let it get to you.

→ Don't get your shirt in a knot.

→ Take it easy / slowly.

→ Calm down.

Consolations

→ The worst is behind you.

→ Things could be a lot worse.

→ You'd be best to put it all behind you.

→ You're out of the woods now.

→ Just chalk it up to experience.

Comfort and Condolences

→ I'm sorry for your loss.

→ My deepest sympathies / my condolences.

→ My heart goes out to you.

→ My thoughts are with you.

→ I'll be thinking of you.

Humoring Someone

When problems get the better of you, or you make them bigger than they are, it may be necessary to see the brighter side of things. Humor can often be the best medicine. If, however, the person you're trying to help is merely feeling sorry for him- or herself, he or she might need a reality check.

→ What doesn't kill you only makes you stronger.

→ It's not the end of the world.

→ Things are never as bad as they seem.

→ Some day you'll look back and laugh.

→ You'll get over it in no time.

→ You'll live.

→ Look on the bright side.

→ Lighten up.

→ Chill out.

Putting Things in Perspective

→ Don't make a mountain out of a molehill.

→ Don't take it so seriously / to heart.

→ Don't get carried away.

→ How about coming back to earth?

→ Get over it!

→ Get real / a grip!

When Advice Is Ignored

Although we mean well, sometimes people don't take or appeciate the advice we give.

→ Don't come running to me.

→ It's your business / funeral.

→ It's up to you.

→ Suit yourself.

Reluctance and Avoidance

Depending on the circumstances, it is not always easy or desirable to talk about a problem. Sometimes you may not completely understand where the problem comes from or you may not be ready to talk.

Not Knowing the Source of the Problem

➜ I haven't a clue / the faintest idea / the foggiest idea.

➜ I can't put my finger on it.

➜ I don't know what's wrong.

➜ Your guess is as good as mine.

➜ You got me stumped / beat.

➜ Don't ask me.

➜ Beats me!

Avoiding a Problem

➜ I'd rather not discuss it.

➜ I don't feel like talking about it.

➜ It's not your problem / concern / business.

➜ I don't see the issue / the problem / what's wrong.

➜ What's the big deal?

➜ Leave me alone.

➜ Let it be.

➜ Back off, why don't you?

Expressing Emotions

Worry and Fear

➜ This problem has me worried / concerned / upset.

➜ That really freaks me out.

→ I'm very worried / concerned / upset / uptight.

→ I'm a bundle of nerves.

→ I'm just sick with worry / fear.

→ I'm beside myself.

→ I'm afraid / frightened / scared / freaking out.

Embarrassment and Shame

→ I'm embarrassed / mortified about my bad memory.

→ I could die of shame / embarrassment.

→ There's no way I can show my face.

→ I'm the laughing stock of our class.

→ I'm so ashamed of myself.

→ I wish the earth would swallow me up.

→ I've got egg on my face.

Anger

→ I'm really angry / mad / furious / ticked off / pissed off about my marks.

→ My roommate really ticked / cheesed / pissed me off.

→ Rush-hour traffic really bugs / annoys / bothers me.

→ What really gets me is the way people ignore the rules.

→ That rude saleslady's attitude burns me up.

→ I've had it / had it up to here with long lines!

→ I'm so angry at my brother I could scream!

→ My son is really pushing my buttons.

→ I'm losing it / flipping out / going off the deep end!

Sadness

→ I'm feeling blue / out of sorts / down / down in the dumps / down in the mouth.

→ Jeanne's beside herself with grief.

→ Gabriel's broken-hearted.

→ I just can't snap out of it.

→ I feel so bad / so sad I could cry.

Dialogue: What's the Matter?

Underline or highlight the phrases from the chapter.

Jamie: Katie, want to go out with the gang?

Katie: I'm sorry if I sound like a party pooper but I'm just not in the mood.

Jamie: You sure haven't been your cheery self lately. Is anything the matter?

Katie: Well, ever since our boss announced that the company's up for sale, everybody's on edge, including me.

Jamie: I can understand that. Nobody likes uncertainty, that's for sure.

Katie: Especially when you might end up without a job.

Jamie: That's really too bad. So, what's the story?

Katie: It's all because the management got carried away and took on too much debt.

Jamie: How long has this been going on?

Katie: For some time as it turns out. I'm worried sick about my job and furious at the same time.

Jamie: Well, if I were you, I wouldn't freak out. With your qualifications, you shouldn't have any trouble finding another job.

Katie: But I don't want another job. And Jamie, this is just between you and me.

Jamie: I won't breathe a word. And Katie, don't worry. Things always have a way of working out.

Katie: That's easy for you to say. It's not happening to you.

Jamie: I guess life just never is a bowl of cherries.

Katie: You're telling me. It seems like everything's happening at once.

Jamie: Why, is something else wrong?

Katie: Yeah, I'm having trouble with my stupid car, and I can't really afford any big repairs right now.

Jamie: I know a reasonable mechanic. How about if I have him take a look?

Katie: Thanks, Jamie, but what's the use?

Jamie: Or I could lend you some money if you'd like.

Katie: What good would that do when I already owe enough on my credit cards?

Jamie: Well, I tried but I guess I'm no Doctor Phil,* am I?

---

*① Dr. Phil McGraw is a popular television personality, psychologist, and author who is known for his frank advice.

Katie: You're a good shoulder to cry on, and I really appreciate it, Jamie. Look, why don't you go out without me?

Jamie: What fun would that be? Anyway, now that you've got a few things off your chest, I still think it'd do you good to take your mind off everything.

Katie: How? With ice cream? A feel-good movie? Some fresh air?

Jamie: I tell you what. Let's walk over to the park and stop for ice cream on the way back.

Katie: Now, you're talking. I feel better already.

Topics for Practice

Talk about a recent problem you've had:

1. at work or school;
2. with your health or physical fitness;
3. with your family or friends;
4. with your car or computer;
5. with money;
6. that was caused by a mistake or an accident;
7. that you needed help with;
8. that you were able to solve on your own;
9. that wasn't as bad as it seemed;
10. that you were worried about.

What advice would you give to someone who:

1. wants to stop smoking;
2. is unhappy at work or school;
3. has gained too much weight;
4. had a fight or disagreement with a friend or loved one;
5. wants to make friends in a new city or town;
6. has trouble saving money;
7. is homesick;
8. is upset because he or she didn't get a job he or she really wanted;
9. is nervous about flying;
10. often has bad headaches?

Vocabulary Notes

_____

_____

_____

_____

_____

_____

_____

_____

_____

_____

_____

_____

_____

_____

_____

_____

_____

_____

_____

CHAPTER 6

Decisions and Goals

Objectives

- to explore options and talk about decisions
- to make plans and set schedules
- to set goals and recognize achievements

When Pavel emigrated from Russia to the United States two years ago, he participated in an intermediate English course for new-comers. He adjusted quickly to his new environment, and, because of his background, he was hired by an engineering company with strong business ties in Eastern Europe.

Pavel reads extensively to broaden his vocabulary, and in his spare time he plays squash and soccer at a local sports club. He is comfortable speaking English on an everyday basis and has little trouble translating from English into his native Russian when necessary. His main concern is that he won't be able to participate confidently in the kind of planning, goal setting, and decision-making for which his team is responsible, and he worries that his language skills might not live up to his project leader's expectations.

Once you have defined a problem, as in Chapter 5, you will need to make decisions about the things you want to buy or acquire; the changes you intend to make at work, school, or home; or the goals you hope to achieve through future endeavors. While you are sometimes faced with making decisions and plans on your own, most frequently your conversations will include family, friends, or coworkers whose input you need to take into consideration.

Phrases

Openers: What Are We Going to Do?

→ We need to make a decision / to do something about the problem / situation / issue.

→ What are our options / choices / alternatives / possibilities?

→ What choice / option / alternative / solution do we have?

→ What can we do about this situation / issue / problem?

→ How does this appeal / sound to you?

→ How can we go about this?

→ The situation calls for a decision.

Options and Alternatives

Once you have identified the issues, you can go about exploring your options. Hopefully you can make a choice, but sometimes you may find that under the circumstances you have no choice at all.

Situation: Maria and Pablo need a second car. Although they'd like to buy a brand new one, they can't afford to, and they don't really want to go into debt.

Options

→ We **could always** buy a used car.

→ **One option / choice / possibility** would be to buy a used car.

→ **Perhaps / maybe** we should consider / look at buying a used car.

→ **Wouldn't it be smarter** to buy a used car?

→ We could **keep** a used car **in mind**.

Alternatives

→ **Rather than / instead of** buying a used car, we could lease a new one.

→ **As an alternative / alternatively** we could lease a new car.

→ **Another option / choice** would be to lease a new car.

No Choice

→ We **have no alternative / choice / option but** to wait and save our money.

→ **Our options are limited to** waiting and saving our money.

→ We **can't do anything except** wait and save our money.

→ **Our only option / choice / possibility** is to wait and save our money.

→ **The best we can do at this point** is wait and save our money.

Reasons and Purpose

Before you can make a decision or set a goal, you need to clarify the reasons behind your situation and determine the purpose your course of action will serve.

Situation: Maximilian would like to apply for a more challenging job, but the companies he's interested in prefer candidates who are fluent in both spoken and written English.

Stating a Reason

→ **Because / since** companies are looking for candidates fluent in English, I need to improve my English.

→ **Because of / due to** a competitive job market, I need to improve my English.

→ Companies are looking for fluent speakers of English. **As a result / consequently / therefore** I have to improve my English.

→ **The reason** I need to improve my English is that companies are looking for fluent speakers.

→ **My motivation / incentive** for improving my English is a better job.

Stating a Purpose

→ I'm going to the United States **for*** English lessons / **to** get more experience.

→ I'm going to the United States **so / so that** I can improve my English.

→ I'm going to spend a year in the United States **to / in order to / so as to** improve my English.

→ I'm going to the United States for a year **because** I want to improve my English.

→ **The purpose of / the point in** going to the United States is to improve my English.

Asking About Reasons or Purpose

→ **Why** are you going to the United States for a year?

→ **What** are you going to the United States **for**?

→ **What's behind** your going to the United States?

---

*ⓘ **For** is followed by a noun, whereas **to** in the case of expressing purpose is not a preposition, but the infinitive form of a verb: **to do / to be / to learn**, etc.

→ **How come** you're going to the United States?*

→ **What are your reasons for** going to the United States?

→ **What reason do you have for** going to the United States?

→ **What purpose will** going to the United States **serve**?

→ **What's your motivation / purpose / incentive in** going to the United States?

Advantages and Disadvantages

Making decisions involves not only making comparisons and contrasts, as outlined in Chapter 4, but also taking a good look at the advantages and disadvantages each choice has to offer.

Situation: Eriko and Mun-Jung are living with a homestay family in the suburbs. Although they get along with their hosts, they would like more privacy and independence so they're thinking about moving to an apartment downtown.

Advantages

→ **The advantages / benefits / merits / assets** of downtown are its central location and convenience.

→ **The pros** are location and convenience.

→ The convenience of downtown can be **a blessing / a bonus**.

→ **A strong point / good thing** is the central location.

---

*① When you ask a question beginning with **How come,** you do not invert the subject and verb.

→ Downtown's central location and convenience are **advantageous / beneficial / favorable**.

→ **On the plus / positive side / upside** downtown is central and convenient.

→ The central location and convenience **speak for** downtown.

→ We can **benefit / profit from** the convenient location.

→ The convenient location could **work in our favor**.

Disadvantages

→ The **disadvantages / drawbacks / liabilities** of downtown are the expensive rents and the noise at night.

→ **The cons** are the expensive rents and the noise at night.

→ The noise at night can be **a curse**.

→ **A weak point / bad thing** is the expensive rents.

→ **On the minus / negative side / downside** the rents downtown are more expensive and there's more noise at night.

→ The expensive rents and the noise at night **speak against** downtown.

Adding Information

→ **In addition / additionally / on top of that**, we would have to spend less on public transportation if we lived downtown.

→ **Furthermore / moreover** we'd have to spend less on public transportation.

→ We'd **also** spend less on public transportation.

→ **Not only** would we be closer to shopping, **but** we'd spend less on public transportation.

→ **Along with / as well as** spending less on public transportation, we'd be closer to shopping.

Making a Decision

According to Sophocles, quick decisions are unsafe decisions, which is why decision-making is one of the most difficult things you have to do, especially when it concerns your health, welfare, and money. Often you might prefer to avoid or delay the process, but find you can't when you are facing urgent matters. Decisions can involve a long and painful process of persuasion, compromise, commitment, consensus, and verification, especially when other people are involved. In this case, you may be called upon to make promises as a sign that you will hold up your end of the bargain. Seeing a decision through also requires considerable determination to reach a deal that everyone can live with.

Persuasion

formal   You **have to admit / agree / see that** having your own business makes sense.

Don't you think it's a good / great idea to buy a house?

Doesn't the idea of changing your job **sound** good?

What have you got to lose?

Changing your job **won't hurt / kill you**.

There's nothing to be afraid of.

Think of what you have to gain.

Trust me, it's for the best.

Don't knock it until you've tried it.

Imagine what you'll be missing.

Don't be a stick in the mud / party pooper / a chicken.

informal Oh, come on.

Urgency

→ This is important / urgent / critical / high priority.

→ This is of utmost importance.

→ This is an emergency.

→ It's a matter of life and death.

→ We can't wait on this.

→ There's no time to hesitate / to waste / to fool around.

→ The situation has reached critical mass.

Compromise

➜ I'm sure we can work / figure something out.

➜ We can find / work out a compromise.

➜ Let's meet halfway / in the middle.

➜ We need some give and take / some leeway / some room to move on this.

➜ We can try to find a happy medium.

Checking and Verifying

➜ Can we go over this again?

➜ Can you run that past me again?

➜ Is everybody on the same page?

➜ Do we see eye to eye?

➜ I need to check that once more.

➜ Let's walk through this again.

Defining a Decisive Point

➜ **In the final analysis**, it is money that makes the difference.

➜ **When it comes right down to it**, it's all about money.

➜ **When all's said and done**, it's a matter of money.

➜ **Anyway you look at it**, it's the money that decides.

➜ **It all comes down / boils down to** money.

➜ **The crux of the matter** is money.

➜ **It all depends on** money.

➜ **At the end of the day**, it's all about money.

Stating a Decision

→ I've **decided to** take out a loan / **decided on** taking out a loan.

→ I've **made a decision to** quit my job and go back to school.

→ I've **taken the first step toward** selling my house.

→ I've **made up my mind to** repaint the living room.

→ I've **opted for** a life insurance policy.

→ I'll **have** the steak and lobster.

→ **This is the deal**.

Asking for a Commitment or Consensus

→ Who's for it / in favor?

→ Do I have your support / agreement?

→ Can I count you in on this?

→ Are you a part of this?

→ Are you okay with this?

Making a Commitment

→ You can bank / count on me.

→ I'm in on this / in favor of this.

→ I'll go along with that.

→ I'll back / support you all the way.

→ I'm behind you 100 percent / all the way.

→ You have my vote / pledge / commitment.

Promises

→ I promise / swear to stick to our decision / agreement.

→ I give you my word / word of honor / promise.

→ I will abide by our decision / deal / agreement.

→ I will keep my end of the bargain.

→ You can hold me to it.

→ I won't go back on it.

→ Cross my heart and hope to die.

→ A deal's a deal.

Determination

→ You can't talk me out of this / change my mind / stop me.

→ There's nothing more to discuss.

→ I'm not moving / budging an inch on this.

→ My mind's set / made up.

→ I'm sticking to my guns / with it.

→ I'm doing this come hell or high water.

→ It's a done deal.

→ That's it / final.

Indecision and Hesitation

Sometimes the best decision may be no decision: if you can't say "yes," you have to say "no." While indecision can appear to be procrastination, waiting until the time is right can show prudence.

Indecision

→ You're straddling / sitting on the fence.

→ You're wavering / seesawing / hemming and hawing.

→ I just don't know.

→ I'm not sure about that.

→ I can't say one way or the other.

→ I can't make up my mind.

→ I don't know where I stand.

→ It's debatable.

Hesitating and Delay

→ I need to sleep on it / think it over / mull it over / give it some more thought.

→ Maybe we should take our time / wait and see.

→ I'm having second thoughts / getting cold feet.

→ We should look before we leap.

→ Let's keep it on the back burner.

→ Let's not make any hasty decisions / moves.

→ Tomorrow's another day.

Setting Schedules and Deadlines

It is usual to attach a timeline to a decision; that is, you need to set a time or deadline for when actions have to begin or be completed.

Asking About Deadlines

→ What's our timeline / time horizon / time frame?

→ Are we talking short term or long term?

→ What's the deadline on this?

→ What are we looking at time-wise?

→ When's the first payment due?

→ When does the offer expire?

→ How soon do we have to know?

→ By when / what time does the project have to be completed?

Setting a Date

→ We can **plan / schedule** that **for** tomorrow / next week.

→ I'll **pencil that in for** Tuesday afternoon / April tenth.

→ **Let's set a date for** the party.

→ I'll **make a note of it for** Friday.

→ **A suitable / convenient time** would be sometime next week.

→ The assignment **has to be in** on Monday.

→ We need a decision **by** 2:00 / Friday / next week at the latest.

→ The payment will **be / come due on** the fifteenth.

Future Time

→ **tomorrow / tomorrow** morning / afternoon / evening / night

→ **next** week / month / year

→ **the day after** tomorrow / **the week after** next

→ **the following** Thursday / week / month

→ **in** five minutes / two hours / five days / three months / ten years

→ five minutes / hours / five days / three months / ten years **from now**

→ **by** 9:00 / Thursday / next Friday / October / 2025

Goals and Plans

Setting goals and formulating plans are an integral part of decision-making. Goals not only guide your actions, but the intention to achieve them can motivate and drive you.

Asking About Short-Term Plans

➜ **What are you planning** to do for the summer?

➜ **What are you doing** on the weekend?

➜ **What do you have in mind for** your honeymoon / after graduation?

➜ **What are you going to do about** a job?

➜ **Are you doing anything** after school?

➜ **Got / have any plans for** next year?

Short-Term Plans

➜ **I'm planning / hoping** to travel down the West Coast.

➜ **We're thinking about** building a house.

➜ **I'm going to** move to an island for the summer.

➜ **I intend to** renovate my condo.

Asking About Long-Term Goals

➜ What are your professional **goals / objectives / aims / targets / ambitions**?

➜ **What goals / objectives** do you want to reach in your life?

➜ **What do you hope to** achieve / accomplish in college?

➜ **Where do you want to be** professionally / personally in five years?

→ **What are you aiming to** do in your career / in your private life?

→ **Where do you see** yourself / your business / in five years?

Stating Goals and Plans

→ **My goal / aim / objection / dream / ambition** is to start my own business.

→ **I hope / aspire** to write a book.

→ **I plan to** sail / **plan on** sailing around the world some day.

→ **I dream of** retiring at the age of forty.

→ **It's my dream to** climb Mount Everest.

→ **I'm striving to** make a million dollars / **I'm aiming for** a million dollars.

→ **Our target is to** retire early and travel around the world.

→ **I have my sights set on** an Olympic gold medal.

→ **I'm set on** making a documentary.

→ **My New Year's resolution is to** stop smoking.

Encouragement, Recognition, and Congratulations

When a friend or family member is starting out on a new undertaking, you can support them with words of encouragement, recognition, and congratulations.

Encouragement

➜ You've got what it takes to win the race!

➜ You can handle / do it!

➜ You were cut out for this!

➜ Go on, give it a try / a go / your best shot!

➜ Don't be afraid / give up / quit now.

➜ Keep your chin up!

➜ Knock yourself out!

➜ Never say never!

➜ Break a leg!*

➜ Go for it!

Respect and Recognition

➜ If it hadn't been for you, we wouldn't have been successful.

➜ We all think very highly of you.

➜ We take off our hats to you.

➜ I have to hand it to you.

➜ The credit is all yours.

➜ You've made a great contribution.

➜ You have our respect.

➜ Respect!

➜ Hats off!

---

*ⓘ This expression originated in the theater and means "good luck!"

Congratulations

formal	I'd like to congratulate you on your good marks.
	My congratulations / compliments on your promotion.
	You can be proud of your achievements / accomplishments.
	You've really proven yourself.
	You've done a fine job.
	You deserve / you've earned it!
	What a success / an accomplishment!
	Good job / work!
	Congrats!
	Kudos!
informal	Way to go!

Expressing Emotions

Making a decision can involve your heart as well as your head, so it is useful to know the right words to express emotions such as hope, anticipation, doubt, regret, and disappointment.

Hope

→ I **hope / pray to God** I'll be accepted into medical school.

→ I'm **hopeful / optimistic / positive** about getting a good job.

→ I **trust that** everything will work out for you.

→ I **have high hopes for** our children / **that** our children will go to college.

→ **Hopefully / God willing / with any luck** we'll make a profit on the sale.

→ **I'd like to think that** my kids will do well in college.

→ I'll keep my fingers crossed for you.

Anticipation

→ I **can't wait to** take sailing lessons.

→ I'm **really looking forward to** grad school / to going to grad school.

→ I'm **all wound up about** my new job.

→ I'm on pins and needles (feeling nervous).

→ He's raring to go.

→ He's eager as a beaver.

Doubt

→ I **have serious / grave / nagging doubts about** putting our house up for sale.

→ We're **having second thoughts** about putting our house on the market.

→ I'm **not convinced about** this exercise program / **that** this exercise program is the answer.

→ I **doubt that** we'll sell our house.

→ I **wonder about** putting our house up for sale right now.

→ I'm **not sure / certain about** selling our house in the present market.

→ I **don't know if / whether** we should sell our house.

→ We shall see.

Regret

→ **Had I known / if I'd known** that the laptop was going on sale, I'd have waited to buy it.

→ I **wish** I had thought of applying for a visa earlier.

→ I **regret** not putting more effort into my studies at school.

→ I'm **sorry about** wasting my money.

→ **Next time** I'll be more careful.

→ I could kick myself.

Disappointment

→ I was **really looking forward to** the yoga class / taking the yoga class.

→ I **had my heart / mind set on** getting a promotion.

→ The exhibition **let me down**.

→ My partner **left me in the lurch**.

→ I'm crushed / devastated / blown away.

→ I had my hopes up.

Dialogue: A Tough Decision

Underline or highlight the phrases from the chapter.

Gina: Are you doing anything this weekend, Josh?

Josh: Nothing exciting. The deadline for community college registration is approaching fast, and I still haven't made up my mind which course to take.

Gina: What are your options?

Josh: Well, I've been debating whether to take a course on how to build a basic website or one on personal financial fundamentals.

Gina: That's a tough choice. I guess it all boils down to which one meets your goals.

Josh: My long-term goal is to start up my own business.

Gina: Good for you!

Josh: The advantage of being able to build your own website is that I can get myself out there on the Internet.

Gina: For sure. There's so much you can do on the web. A friend of mine sells the jewelry she makes online, and she's doing great.

Josh: On the other hand, I need to know how to manage my finances.

Gina: Hmm. Sounds like six of one, and half a dozen of the other.

Josh: I've even considered taking both courses at the same time.

Gina: You're a bright guy, Josh. Go for it!

Josh: The downside, however, is I'd have to fork out a lot of money at once. I'm not a millionaire yet.

Gina: I suppose going into debt in order to learn how to manage your money would be defeating the purpose. There isn't a compromise, is there?

Josh: No, it's one or the other. Anyway, enough about me. Got any plans yourself?

Gina: Yeah, guess what? I enrolled in the Herbal Studies Certificate Program.

Josh: How come? I thought you intended to go to med school.

Gina: My parents have their heart set on me becoming a doctor, but holistic healing and alternative therapy are more up my alley. And the good thing about the course is it's really hands-on. I can hardly wait!

Josh: I wish I was as enthusiastic. And decisive. The more I think about it the harder it gets.

Gina: Maybe you shouldn't think about it so much.

Josh: Yeah, but I don't want to make a decision I'll regret.

Gina: In any case, you have to trust yourself, listen to your inner voice.

Josh: Right now all I hear from the inside is my stomach growling.

Gina: Then, let's go to my family's restaurant. My grandpa always said never make a hard decision on an empty stomach.

Josh: Sounds like a wise man. Was he a judge?

Gina: No, a cook. He started the business.

Topics for Practice

Talk about a recent decision you've made:

1. about work or school;
2. about a holiday or trip;
3. about your money;

4. about how you voted in the last election;
5. about something you wanted or needed to buy;
6. that was very difficult to make;
7. that was very easy to make;
8. that involved your friends or family;
9. that required you to do some research;
10. that you regret or wish you could change.

Talk about your goals or plans:

1. for your career or job;
2. for your family;
3. for your next vacation;
4. for your health;
5. for your retirement;
6. for a team, club, or organization you belong to;
7. for the next five / ten / twenty years;
8. to change something in your life;
9. to do something you've always dreamed of;
10. to learn something you've never had time for.

Vocabulary Notes

PART 2

Phrases for Discussions

"Our opinions do not really blossom into fruition until we have expressed them to someone else."

—Mark Twain

CHAPTER 7

Opinions

Objectives

- to express your opinion and to ask others for their opinions
- to agree or disagree with an opinion
- to support an opinion with facts, statistics, and examples

Marie-Claire has been accepted into a graduate program at a U.S. university where she will continue her journalism studies. She is well aware of how difficult it will be to make her way in such a competitive field as television journalism. Even if she's lucky enough to land a job in her native country of France, she will not go as far as she hopes to in a global environment without advanced English skills.

While still in school Marie-Claire attended intensive summer courses in England and traveled widely with her family throughout Europe. She has become a competent translator, but good academic skills are not enough for her. In order to participate in research projects, to conduct investigative interviews, to make convincing arguments in both speaking and writing, and to exchange and challenge opinions in discussions of current affairs, Marie-Claire must master idiomatic phrases and employ them with the ease of a native English speaker.

Everyone has an opinion, and in cultures that value freedom of speech people voice their opinions on an array of subjects ranging from the trivial (the weather, traffic) to more serious topics (education, health) to controversial issues (global warming, capital punishment, stem-cell research).

Giving an opinion can be easy, particularly if you "jump on the bandwagon" and echo popular public opinion or repeat views you hear or read in the news, on television, or at home. Being able to express an informed opinion and to make a convincing argument supported by facts is a significant achievement in a second language.

Phrases

Openers: Asking for an Opinion

→ **What do you think about** the city's plan to replace the old bridge?

→ **What do you make of** the new cafeteria?

→ **What's your opinion of / on** the school's food services?

→ **What's your view / take / stand / position on** the changes to our curriculum?

→ **Where do you stand on** drunk-driving laws?

→ **How do you feel about** the recent weather?

→ **What's your reaction to** the President's speech?

→ **I'd like to hear what you think about** the education system.

→ **I'd like an honest opinion on** my presentation.

Stating an Opinion

An opinion can be stated in a personal way by showing personal ownership—that is, it is your opinion and you want to stress that. You can also give an opinion in the form of an

(i) Look at the *Letters to the Editor* or editorials in your local newspaper to see how people express their views on current issues.

impersonal statement by putting forward what someone should or shouldn't do about a particular issue.

➜ I **think / feel / believe / find that** the old bridge should be repaired instead of replaced.

➜ I **support / favor / advocate / stand for / oppose** electronic surveillance.

➜ I'm **convinced that** guns don't belong in people's homes.

➜ I'm **for / against / opposed to** universal health care.

➜ **My opinion / position / stand / viewpoint on** spanking is that it should be a parent's right.

➜ **In my opinion / view** smoking should / shouldn't be allowed in restaurants and bars.

➜ **From my point of view / perspective** bullying in school shouldn't be tolerated.

➜ **As far as I'm concerned** the city should / shouldn't set up a needle exchange downtown.

➜ **If you ask me,** the price of gasoline is outrageous.

➜ **The way I look at it** sports has become too much like a business.

➜ **As I see it / the way I see things** good manners should be taught in school.

➜ **It seems / appears to me that** children are losing touch with nature.

➜ **Someone / they should do something about** homelessness.

The following is a list of adverbs that can add strength or conviction to your opinions:

absolutely / completely / entirely / firmly / fully

definitely / for sure / without a doubt

frankly / honestly / personally

strongly / unequivocally

Examples:

I **firmly** believe that all children should be given equal educational opportunities.

Without a doubt the city needs a more efficient public-transportation system.

We **strongly** support zero tolerance for drinking and driving.

Value Judgments

Value judgments are biased opinions based on personal beliefs rather than facts or reliable information. Usually value judgments are statements of what is good or bad, and they are colored by cultural or religious background, individual preferences, and experiences. Because people cannot be objective and rational all of the time, they often make value judgments and take them for informed opinions.

Value judgments tell us more about the person who makes them than the subject he or she is discussing. Although it is difficult not to make value judgments, you should avoid them in formal discussions and debates where objectivity and rational thinking are required.

Examples:

Jonathan is the best teacher in the school.

Drinking too much alcohol is bad for you.

Soccer hooligans are a bunch of Neanderthals.

Generalizations

As well as avoiding value judgments, you should be careful not to make hasty or sweeping generalizations. For example, it is a sweeping generalization to say that, because a woman caused an accident, all women are bad drivers, when there are of course many women who are excellent drivers.

In order to be valid, general statements must be substantiated by repeated experience and accepted as common knowledge.

→ **Everyone knows / it is common knowledge that** obesity increases the risk of heart disease.

→ **In general / generally speaking** obesity increases the risk of heart disease.

→ Obesity **usually** / **generally** / **commonly** / **more often than not** increases the risk of heart disease.

→ **As a rule** obesity increases the risk of heart disease.

→ Obesity **tends to** increase the risk of heart disease.

→ **In the majority of cases** obesity increases the risk of heart disease.

Agreeing and Disagreeing

Asking for Agreement

→ Which opinion do you support / side with / agree with?

→ Which side of the argument are you on?

→ What do you say to that?

→ Who do you agree with?

→ Do you agree / disagree?

→ Do you concur or not?

→ Do you see it my way?

→ Are we in agreement?

→ Are you with me?

Agreeing

formal   I agree with you completely / fully / absolutely / entirely.

I couldn't agree with you more!

My thoughts / feelings / opinion exactly.

You're right / absolutely right about that!

You've hit the nail on the head.

You took the words right out of my mouth.

You can say that again.

I hear you!

You said it!

Hear, hear!

Right on!

informal   Totally!

Disagreeing

formal   I disagree completely / totally / absolutely!

I can't share your opinion / view at all.

I have to / beg to differ.

I don't see it that way at all.

That's easy for you to say.

You've got that all wrong.

That's ridiculous / baloney!

That makes no sense.

informal   No way!

Indifference

→ I don't know what to make of the whole issue.

→ It doesn't matter to me one way or the other.

→ It's six of one and half a dozen of the other.

→ It's not worth getting excited about.

→ It's all the same to me.

→ I couldn't care less.

Supporting an Opinion

A convincing argument requires the support of facts, figures, and examples. Otherwise, an unfounded opinion can come across in a discussion as bias, prejudice, or just hot air.

A fact is something that is definitely known to be true. Without the support of facts, an opinion is neither substantiated nor convincing. Be careful to distinguish between proven and probable facts:

■ Proven facts are accepted and indisputable.

   Example: The earth revolves around the sun.

■ Probable facts sound reasonable and are probably true, but haven't been proven.

   Example: The Minister of Health reported in his speech last night that the government has spent 30 percent more on health care this year.

Another danger is that you can probably find as many facts to oppose an argument as you can to support it. A scientific study may be convincing, but as you continually hear in the news, researchers come up with new findings that can contradict previous results. In the end, you have to use your judgment and common sense.

Compare the previous value judgments in this chapter with the following facts:

➜ Jonathan has a Bachelor of Education degree and 15 years of teaching experience.

➜ A small amount of alcohol can impair people's judgment and slow their reaction time.

➜ FIFA has taken drastic measures to control aggressive behavior among groups of fans at soccer matches.

Facts

➜ **It's clear / obvious / evident that** the Internet has become a major source of information.

➜ **As a matter of fact / in fact** Internet use is growing worldwide.

➜ **The fact is that** the Internet is a part of our daily life.

➜ **Clearly / obviously** people use the Internet more and more.

➜ **There's no doubt that** the Internet will continue to grow in importance.

➜ **I'd like to point out that** without the Internet, communication would be slower.

Figures and Statistics

Some facts, such as the relationship between obesity and heart disease, can be self-evident; that is, they do not require a detailed explanation to prove their validity. Nevertheless, figures and statistics can be useful when you want to make a strong case for or against an issue. Because studies are being conducted on an ongoing basis, be sure to quote the most recent and reputable ones.

Facts That Express Numbers and Costs

→ The **average** world penetration of mobile cell phone use **stands at** 96.2 percent.

→ **About 13 countries** still do not have access to the Internet.

→ **About 8.6 percent / nearly one-tenth of Internet users** are located in the United States.

→ In Europe **8 out of 10 people** use the Internet.*

→ Patients with an alcohol problem are **nearly five times more likely** to die in motor vehicle crashes, **16 times more likely** to die in falls, and **10 times more likely** to become fire or burn victims.

→ Americans **are subject to $4 billion worth of** alcohol marketing each year.

→ In 2002, alcohol accounted for **more than $14.5 billion in** medical costs, or **$463 per capita**, in Canada.**

---

* Source: http://www.internetworldstats.com/stats9.htm.
** Source: *Alcohol, Trauma and Impaired Driving*, 4th edition, 2009. MADD.

Facts Concerning Trends and Changes

→ The years 2002, 2003, and 2007 were **relatively high** drought years, while 2001, 2005, and 2009 were **relatively low** drought years.

→ Carbon dioxide **accounts for / makes up** approximately 80 percent of this increase.

→ Greenhouse gas emissions **increased by** 17 percent from 1990–2007.

→ The prevalence of extreme single-day precipitation events **remained fairly steady** between 1910 and the 1980s, but **has risen substantially** since then.

→ Many, but not all, human sources of greenhouse gas emissions **are expected to rise** in the future.

→ When examining the entire ACE Index data series from 1950 to 2009, **no clear trends** in cyclone intensity **are apparent**.

→ Over the entire period from 1910 to 2008, the prevalence of extreme single-day precipitation events increased **at a rate of about half a percentage point per** decade.*

Verbs That Express a Change, or Lack of Change

→ grow / rise / increase / climb / surge / skyrocket

→ decrease / reduce / lower / decline / drop / dwindle / fall / sink / plummet

---

* Source: Climate Change Indicators in the United States, EPA, https://www.epa.gov/climatechange/climate-change-basic-information.

→ remain / stay / hold steady / stagnate / show no change / level off / freeze

→ fluctuate / change / vary / go up and down / see-saw

Adverbs That Express a Rate of Change

→ sharply / steeply / dramatically / significantly / measurably / exponentially / suddenly

→ steadily / constantly / consistently / regularly

→ gradually / slowly / little by little / incrementally

→ barely / hardly / minimally / marginally / slightly

Expressing an Inexact Number or Amount

→ about / around / circa / in the neighborhood of / give or take / thereabouts

→ approximately / roughly / nearly / close to / approaching

→ an estimated / projected / adjusted / relative / ball park figure

Vague Language

Watch for words that sound vague and unconvincing.

→ **kind of / sort of / somewhat / more or less** important

→ **a little, a little bit** dangerous

→ He's an expert **or something like that / in a way**.

→ This drug is **a little bit** dangerous if used by children.

Referring to a Source

When you use facts and figures, it is important to refer to your sources. Without a reputable authority to back you up, anything you say can be considered hearsay, and your argument will lack credibility.

→ **According to** a report / interview / an article in the *New York Times* / the *Lancet* . . .

→ **According to** the FDA / the Sierra Club / MADD / UNESCO / Doctor Smith / Professor Jones . . .

→ **A study** / **research** conducted by the University of California / Center for Disease Control and Prevention **shows** / **proves** / **reveals** / **concludes** / **suggests** / **has discovered** / **has determined that** . . .

→ Experts / scientists / researchers say / claim / state / have found that . . .

→ Doctor Smith / Professor Jones has been reported as saying that . . .

→ To quote / cite a well-known / reputable / reliable / credible / expert source . . .

→ A book / article / report said / stated . . .

Common Knowledge

Common knowledge refers to known facts that do not require proof. In other words, we can arrive at these conclusions if we use our common sense.

→ **It is common knowledge / well known that** smoking causes lung disease.

→ **Everybody knows that** smoking increases the risk of lung disease.

→ **As you know**, alcohol consumption impairs one's ability to react quickly in dangerous situations.

Be careful not to confuse myths, urban legends, and popular misconceptions (beliefs that are widespread but unfounded and sometimes blatantly erroneous) with common knowledge that is based on fact. Just because a large number of people believe something to be true doesn't make it true.

Examples of urban myths:

There are deadly alligators living in the New York City sewer system.

You can get high by smoking the inside of a banana peel.

Giving Examples

Giving an example is an effective way to support an opinion and to illustrate a point.

Example:

Take, for example, Michel, who believes that most people are not aware of how much water they waste at home.

→ **Let me offer an example:** a leaky toilet can waste 200 gallons of water per day.

→ **For example / instance** a leaky toilet can waste 200 gallons of water per day.

→ **As an example / that is** a leaky toilet can waste 200 gallons of water per day.

→ **Take, for example,** a leaky toilet, which can waste 200 gallons of water per day.

→ **In the case of** a leaky toilet, up to 200 gallons of water are wasted in a day.

→ **One / another way** we waste up to 200 gallons of water a day is by not fixing a leaky toilet.

→ **In particular** a leaky toilet can waste 200 gallons of water per day.

→ **Let's say** you have a leaky toilet. You can waste up to 200 gallons of water every day.

→ **If** you have a leaky toilet, **then** you can waste up to 200 gallons of water every day.

Identifying Factors and Reasons

→ **The dominant factor** affecting U.S. emissions trends is CO_2 emissions from fossil fuel combustion.

→ **One factor / contributor / reason** for rising CO_2 emissions is the combustion of fossil fuel.

→ Fossil fuel combustion **contributes to / accounts for / is responsible for** rising CO_2 emissions.

→ Rising CO_2 emissions **are attributed to** fossil fuel combustion.

→ **The reason why** CO_2 emissions have risen **is** fossil fuel combustion.

→ Fossil fuels are widely used in combustion. **That's why** CO_2 emissions have risen.

Making an Argument

As your discussion proceeds, you will want to develop your argument by emphasizing or adding points, and persuading others to take your point of view. Look at the following phrases as they could be used in a discussion about drunk driving.

Emphasizing a Point

→ **I'd like to emphasize / stress / point out / repeat / call your attention to the fact that** three out of every ten Americans are involved at least once in their lifetime in alcohol-related accidents.

→ **I have to stress the fact that** ...

→ **Let me tell you / say this again / repeat / reiterate** ...

→ **Let me make it clear / perfectly clear that** ...

Adding a Point

→ In addition / additionally an alarming number of deaths in motor-vehicle accidents are due to drunk driving.

→ Moreover / furthermore . . .

→ A further / an additional point is . . .

→ Also / as well . . .

→ Besides / on top of that . . .

→ Incidentally / by the way / one more thing . . .

→ As it happens . . .

→ I happen to know that . . .

Referring to a Point

→ **In regard / relation / response / reference to** the Zero Tolerance Law, implementation has reduced accidents caused by intoxicated young drivers by a further 11 percent.

→ **Concerning / pertaining to** Zero Tolerance . . .

→ **As far as** the Zero Tolerance Law **goes / is concerned** . . .

→ **When it comes to** Zero Tolerance . . .

Making Qualifications

→ **Depending on your point of view / position / stance / circumstances** penalties for drunk driving are too stiff / lax.

→ **If you take** penalties for drunk driving **into consideration**, there is a great effect / no effect on prevention.

→ Preventing drunk driving **depends on** the penalties.

→ **It all depends on** how stiff penalties are for drunk driving.

→ **It's a matter of** how stiff penalties are for drunk driving.

→ **Relatively speaking**, penalties for drunk driving are too stiff / lax.

Persuasion

→ **You have to admit / recognize / consider that** the facts are indisputable.

→ **You can't ignore / overlook / discount** the facts.

→ **If you really think about it**, you'll have to agree / disagree.

→ **There are many good / valid reasons** to support / oppose drunk driving laws.

→ **Anybody would agree / see / admit that** the facts are convincing.

→ **It only makes sense / stands to reason that** no one should drink and drive.

→ The facts speak for themselves.

Speaking the Truth

→ Frankly / truthfully / candidly / honestly speaking drunk driving is taking your life into your hands.

→ To tell you the truth . . .

→ The truth of the matter is . . .

→ I'm not lying when I say . . .

→ You can believe me when I say . . .

→ Whether you like it or not . . .

→ I swear . . .

Solutions and Recommendations

Without a recommendation or solution to a problem, an opinion is just an opinion.

You can offer solutions and recommendations by:

- making a suggestion (see page 97);
- using modal verbs;
- using other phrases.

Using Modal Verbs

Positive Statements

strong   The government **must** change the law.

↑   The government **has to** change the law.

   The government **needs to** change the law.

↓   The government **ought to** change the law.

mild   The government **should** change the law.

Negative Statements

strong   People **must not** continue to use harmful pesticides.

↑   People **can't** continue to use harmful pesticides.

   People **ought not to** continue to use harmful pesticides.

↓

mild   People **shouldn't** continue to use harmful pesticides.

Other Phrases

→ **We can solve / resolve / take care of** air pollution by reducing fossil fuel consumption.

→ **One solution** to air pollution **would be** to reduce fossil fuel consumption.

→ **One way to solve / to cut down on / to put an end to / to get around** air pollution **would be** to reduce fossil fuel consumption.

→ I **strongly suggest / recommend / propose** reducing fossil fuel consumption / that we reduce fossil fuel consumption.

→ **What we need is** to reduce fossil fuel consumption.

→ **The key to** cleaner air is to reduce fossil fuel consumption.

→ **We need to think outside of the box if** we want to find a real solution.

Calling for Solidarity

→ We need to roll up our shirtsleeves / pull together / pull our weight.

→ We're all in this together / in the same boat.

→ We have to do our part / our share.

→ We can't bury our heads in the sand / stand by and do nothing.

→ Let's act now / do something about it before it's too late.

Expressing Emotions

You are more likely to express an opinion on the basis of how you feel than what you think about an issue. The stronger you feel, the more vocal you become.

Disgust

→ I find racist remarks entirely unacceptable / revolting / disgusting / off-putting.

→ Too much violence in movies really puts me off / turns me off / grosses me out.

→ The food here is gross / revolting / disgusting / sickening.

→ Dirty bathrooms make me sick / nauseated.

→ Cruelty to animals turns my stomach.

Outrage

→ This is incredible / unbelievable / unreal / outrageous!

→ Have you ever heard anything so ridiculous?

→ I can't understand why / how anyone can say / believe / do that!

→ I just don't get it.

→ Can you believe it?

→ What do they think they're doing?

→ Don't make me laugh!

→ Get out of here!

Disbelief

→ You can't be serious!

→ You're pulling my leg / making it up!

→ There's no way on earth!

→ You gotta be kidding / joking!

→ This is pathetic / unbelievable / a joke!

Dialogue: The Best Idea I've Heard So Far

This dialogue imagines a coffee break at the local café. Underline or highlight the phrases from the chapter.

Bob: So, you guys going to the meeting tonight?

Ray: You mean the town-hall meeting about the new resort they want to build near Coral Beach?

Tom: The way I look at it a resort's just what we need.

Bob: I disagree. The last thing we need is something that'll only make money for a handful of strangers.

Ray: Well, if you ask me, a resort would bring a lot of business into the community. As a matter of fact, that marine resort at Bedford Harbour increased tax revenues by more than 25 percent.

Tom: We all know this town could use a boost like that.

Ray: I couldn't agree with you more. As it is there just aren't enough jobs to keep our young people here.

Bob: I'm not so sure a resort's the answer. I mean most of the jobs are seasonal, low-paying service jobs.

Tom: In my opinion a seasonal job's better than no job. Besides tourists need cafés and restaurants, and that means business opportunities.

Bob: Yeah, but you can't live off the tourists in the winter. Joe, what's your take on this?

Joe: Quite frankly it doesn't really matter much what any of us think.

Ray: What do you mean, Joe?

Joe: The way I see it, the decision's already made. Those developers have got the town council in their pocket, and this meeting's just a way to make everybody think they've got a say.

Bob: Regardless, I'm going to the meeting anyway. Somebody's got to speak out.

Ray: Good point, Bob. After all, it is a free country.

Tom: Well if it were up to me, I'd give it the green light. It's time we started looking forward instead of backward.

Ray: You said it, Tom. It seems every time somebody comes up with a new idea, everybody's against it.

Joe: C'mon, you guys. Remember our cost of living will go up as well.

Tom: And so will property values. I don't have anything against the value of my house going up, do you guys?

Ray: Let me give you a good example. I know a couple in Bedford Harbour who sold their house for five times what they paid for it. You have to agree that's a pretty good return.

Joe: But that also means it costs five times more for a young couple to buy a house, and how many young people can afford that?

Ray: What did I say? Some people just can't look on the bright side.

Joe: What they should do instead is make the Coral Beach area into a park.

Tom: Get real, Joe. We need jobs, not parks.

Jan: Sorry to interrupt, but it looks like you guys could use some more coffee.

Bob: Now Jan, that's the best idea I've heard so far.

Topics for Practice

What's your opinion of:

1. gambling;
2. women in the military;
3. divorce;
4. cosmetic surgery;
5. school uniforms;
6. extreme sports;
7. electric cars;
8. binge drinking;
9. foreign exchange programs for high-school students;
10. tattoos?

How would you ask someone his or her opinion on:

1. using cell phones in cars;
2. customer service in department stores;
3. fast-food restaurants;

4. violence in movies;

5. testing cosmetics on animals;

6. recycling;

7. public transportation;

8. living together before marriage;

9. advertising on television;

10. Internet dating?

Do you agree or disagree with the following opinions?

1. Children should learn a foreign language at an early age.

2. The voting age should be lowered to 16.

3. People who are caught driving when they are drunk should lose their license for life.

4. People who collect welfare should have to do some kind of job to earn the money they receive from the government.

5. Stopping climate change is the responsibility of industry.

6. Cars that run on gasoline should be phased out in favor of cars that use electricity, solar power, and other alternative fuels.

7. Religion should not be taught in public schools.

8. Parents should not be allowed to spank their children.

9. It is dangerous for children to use the Internet.

10. The Olympic Games have become too commercial.

Vocabulary Notes

_____

_____

_____

_____

_____

_____

_____

_____

_____

_____

_____

_____

_____

_____

_____

_____

_____

_____

_____

_____

_____

_____

_____

CHAPTER 8

Group Discussions

Objectives

- ■ to lead and manage a group discussion
- ■ to participate in a group discussion

An experienced software developer with a strong management background, Abdulaziz has been promoted to the position of business development and solutions manager in a specialist recruitment consultancy. In this challenging position Abdulaziz will have the opportunity to use his management and communication skills to lead an international team of IT and software developers, and to build crucial links with a broad network of partners in North and South America, Europe, the Middle East, Africa, and Asia Pacific.

During his studies in the United States, Abdulaziz developed a solid command of technical English and he is conversant in business terms. Now that he will be co-coordinating and conducting workshops, seminars, planning sessions, and business discussions primarily in English, Abdulaziz needs a broader range of phrases in order to keep his team on track and to consult with senior management.

Group discussions are an integral part of your daily communication on all levels: personal, business, and political. Through meaningful discussions, you not only exchange ideas and formulate solutions, but you have the opportunity to test them out on others and receive valuable feedback.

Phrases

Openers: Opening the Floor

formal   I now call the meeting to order.

I'd like to welcome everyone to our meeting / discussion.

I'll begin by thanking everyone for coming / attending / being here.

I'm glad you could all be here today.

Nice to see everyone / all of you.

Shall we begin?

informal   **Let's get** going / started / the ball rolling.

Leading a Discussion

Without a capable leader, a group discussion can easily become a free-for-all that ends in frustration and dissension. To assure that time is used productively and that all participants contribute in a respectful and meaningful way, a skillful leader should be able to:

- provide background information, including facts about the situation or problem to be discussed;
- give everyone adequate and equal chance to speak;
- field and direct questions;
- limit the time individuals speak and prevent one person from monopolizing the discussion or interrupting unnecessarily;
- keep participants on topic;
- ask speakers to support their opinions with facts or arguments and to explain a point that others may not understand;
- ask for agreement or disagreement from other participants where necessary;
- summarize at intervals or have one of the participants summarize the main points discussed so far;
- take a vote on matters that require a decision or motion;
- guide participants in arriving at a conclusion or consensus.

Setting the Topic

→ Today we're going to discuss / talk about the upcoming trade fair.

→ We're here today to discuss the matter of . . .

→ Now that everyone's here, let's get down to the business of . . .

→ As you know, this meeting has been called to discuss . . .

→ Our topic for today's discussion is . . .

Background Information

→ **We'll begin with** the minutes of the last meeting / a summary of our last discussion / a rundown of what's happened since last time.

→ **Our last / previous discussion / meeting concluded with** the decision to change our website.

→ Before we get started, **let me give you an update on** our sales campaign.

→ As you all know, **last time we discussed / talked about / went over** the new schedule . . .

Giving a Speaker the Floor

formal   Who would like to begin / to open the discussion / to have the first word / to go first?

Natalia, would you please state your opinion / position?

First / now / next let's hear from Kevin.

> Let's turn things / the floor over to Yuichiro.
>
> It's your turn now, Chae-Rin.
>
> Veronica, you can take over now.

informal   Go ahead, Costas.

Asking for Comments

➜ Who has something to say to that last remark / comment / point?

➜ Does anyone else have anything to say / to add / to contribute?

➜ Who would like to make a comment?

➜ Any further comments / points / remarks?

➜ Comments, anyone?

Fielding Questions

formal   Would someone like to ask / to pose a question?

Who has a question / would like to ask a question?

Does anyone have a question?

Are there any questions / further questions?

Any questions?

informal   Questions, anyone?

Asking for Responses to Questions

➜ Who'd like to answer / take / respond to the question?

➜ Does anyone have an answer / response?

→ Could I have a response / reply to the question?

→ Let's have some feedback on the last point.

→ Any comments?

Participating in a Group Discussion

As a participant in a group discussion, each member should:

- try to make points clearly and concisely;
- wait his/her turn to speak without interrupting unnecessarily;
- avoid monopolizing the discussion even if he/she has a lot to say on the topic;
- respect other people's opinions and their right to these opinions;
- respect the role of the leader and try not to take over.

Stating a Position

See Stating an Opinion, page 147, for more phrases.

Referring to Other Participants' Points

→ As you said / put it / mentioned . . .

→ According to your opinion / your comment / what you've just said . . .

→ To refer to your last comment / point . . .

Asking a Question

formal   If I may, I'd like to ask Deniz / the last speaker a
               question.

               I was wondering if Inge could answer my question.

               I'd like to ask Lin if / how / why / what …

               Could Jens tell me if / how / why … ?

               My question to Elena is …

informal   I have a question for Tomasz.

Introducing an Opposing Argument

➜ What you said may be possible / true, but if you look at /
consider the facts …

➜ I understand your position, but don't you think …

➜ I agree in principle, but you should consider …

➜ Your point is well taken, but …

➜ That's a valid point, but …

➜ I see your point, but …

➜ On the other hand …

Making Contradictions

➜ Your statement / remark clearly contradicts the evidence.

➜ I'm afraid I have to contradict / challenge you on this.

➜ If you look at the facts you'll see that the opposite / the
contrary is true.

→ Didn't you know / weren't you aware that the facts prove otherwise / the opposite?

→ That's wrong / false / just not the case.

→ Contrary to what you said . . .

→ On the contrary . . .

Making Objections

mild

I question / doubt / have my doubts / wonder about raising prices.

I'm not so sure / convinced of / 100 percent with you on that.

I have to object / take exception to / take issue with that.

That's irrelevant / unrelated / of no consequence / beside the point / begging the question.

That's impossible / incredible / unbelievable / ridiculous / out of the question.

I've never heard anything so ridiculous / absurd / preposterous.

You can't mean that / be serious / expect me to believe that.

You've got to be kidding!

Now, just wait a minute.

strong

No way!

Criticizing Your Opponent

→ It is clear / obvious to us that you are unable to see the difference between . . .

→ I'm afraid you lack a clear understanding of the importance of . . .

→ You don't seem to grasp / realize the full importance of . . .

→ How can you possibly propose / believe such an idea?

→ Don't you think you should be more open-minded?

→ Don't be unfair.

Asking for Justification

→ I don't know / see / understand how you've come up with that.

→ On what grounds do you make that assumption?

→ How did you come up with / arrive at / figure that?

→ Where did you get that idea / those facts?

→ What reason do you have to say that?

→ Why do you think so?

→ How come?

Responding to a Point or Question

→ If I may, I'd like to answer / respond / reply to the question / make a comment.

→ I'd like to address the point / the issue by saying that . . .

→ There's something I'd like to say in response.

→ I want to / need to make something clear . . .

Redirecting a Question

→ What / how about you?

→ And you?

→ Yourself?

Interruptions

At some point in the discussion you may want to add a point or ask a question while someone else is speaking. Instead of butting in, there are phrases that you can use to interrupt politely and respectfully. On the other hand, there may be occasions when you need to be more direct.

Interrupting (Participants)

polite ↑

If you'll excuse / forgive me for interrupting, I'd like to say something.

If you don't mind, there's something I'd like / I need to say.

If I may, I'd just like to say that . . .

I hate to stop you / interrupt like this, but . . .

I don't mean to interrupt / to be rude, but . . .

May I jump in / just say a word?

Sorry to interrupt, but . . .

Excuse me, but . . .

Can I get a word in edgewise here?

brusque   Now, wait a minute.

Reacting to Interruptions (Participants)

polite   Would you be so kind as to let me finish / get to the point?

Would you mind if I finished?

If you could wait, I'll finish / make my point.

Just let me finish.

Hear me out first.

I wasn't finished.

Do you mind?

Don't butt in!

brusque   Stay out of this!

Handling Interruptions (Leader)

polite   If you don't mind, the speaker hasn't finished / made his or her point.

If I could just ask you to wait a moment / to give the speaker a chance to finish.

We'll get back to you, but first let's hear what Andreas has to say.

Please wait your turn / let the speaker finish.

I'm afraid it's not your turn.

brusque

Just hold on.

Quiet, please.

You're out of turn / out of order.

That's enough out of you.

Clarification and Explanations

Asking for Clarification

polite

I'm sorry, but I don't understand / follow / get it / know what you mean.

I'm afraid I'm not quite with you.

Do you think you could go over that again?

Could you please explain what you mean?

Could you run through that again?

What are you getting at / driving at / trying to say?

What has that got to do with it / anything?

What do you mean?

Run that past me again.

brusque

You lost me there!

Giving Clarification

→ What I mean / meant to say is we need to cut costs to stay competitive.

→ What I'm trying to say / to get at is . . .

→ This is how I see it . . .

→ I was really trying to say . . .

→ Let me clear this up / make this perfectly clear . . .

→ It's as clear as / as plain as day.

→ Anyone can see that . . .

Asking for Explanations

polite   I'm sorry, but I didn't understand / don't follow / don't know what you mean.

Could you explain / clarify / elaborate on that?

Could you be more explicit / specific / exact?

Can you give us an explanation / an example?

What are you implying / getting at / talking about?

What do you mean?

What on earth are you talking about?

brusque   For instance?

Giving Explanations

→ Let me explain / put it differently / rephrase that.

→ To begin with this . . .

→ First of all . . .

→ For one thing / for another . . .

→ It's like this . . .

→ That is to say . . .

→ Namely . . .

(See Giving Examples, page 159, for more phrases.)

Rephrasing

→ What I mean to / intended to say is . . .

→ Let me put it this way . . .

→ By this / that I mean . . .

→ In other words . . .

→ Another way to look at it . . .

Misunderstandings

Asking for Repetition

→ Would you please repeat that / say that again / speak up / slow down?

→ Do you think you could repeat that / go over that again?

→ Could you run through that again?

→ I'm afraid we missed that / couldn't hear / didn't catch that.

→ I beg your pardon.

→ Pardon me.

> (i) Depending on the tone of voice, *Pardon me* or *I beg your pardon* can also mean *I don't believe what I'm hearing* and indicates that the speaker is shocked, offended, or surprised.

Not Understanding

→ What are you getting at?

→ I think I'm missing something here.

→ That doesn't seem to make sense.

→ I'm afraid I don't understand.

→ That's beyond me / over my head / all Greek to me.

→ I can't make heads or tails of this.

→ I haven't got the foggiest / faintest idea.

→ I don't get / didn't get that at all.

→ Can you say / put that in plain English?

Checking for Understanding

formal	Has everyone understood?
↑	Is everyone clear / okay on this?
	You know what I mean?
	Know what I'm saying?
	You get my drift?
↓	Got it?
informal	Clear?

Confirming Understanding

→ So, what you're saying is this: the bridge will be closed for another six months!

→ So let me see if I've got this right . . .

→ So what you've said in fact is . . .

→ I take it / gather / assume that . . .

→ I understand / see / get it / hear you loud and clear.

→ I get the message / picture / idea / drift.

→ I see where you're coming from / you're going with this.

→ Right / all right.

Clearing Up a Misunderstanding

formal   That wasn't quite what I said / meant / intended to
             say / wanted to say.

             That wasn't exactly my point / message / intention.

             You've totally misunderstood / misinterpreted what I
             said.

             You've got the wrong idea / missed the point / got
             me all wrong.

             You're putting words in my mouth / twisting my words.

             You're barking up the wrong tree.

informal   I said no such thing!

Managing the Discussion

When the discussion gets going, the leader will want to make sure
that participants stay focused and on track and that not everyone
talks at once. In the event of a heated discussion, a good leader
may have to calm down participants and restore order.

Focusing on the Main Issue

→ The main / primary / real problem / issue / concern is how
   to raise more money.

→ The essence / crux of the matter / most important
   thing is . . .

→ It all comes down to . . .

→ The bottom line is . . .

Getting Attention

→ If you'll excuse me / lend me an ear / pay attention for a moment.

→ Could I have your attention, please?

→ Would everyone stop talking for a moment?

→ Now everyone, listen to / hear this.

→ Attention, everybody!

→ Listen up!

→ Quiet now!

Getting Back on Track

formal   We seem to have gotten off track / off topic.

I'd like to bring the discussion back to our topic.

Perhaps we could get back to the main point.

Let's not get sidetracked / off on the wrong track.

Can we get back to / stick to the point?

You're changing the subject.

That's beside the point / irrelevant / off track.

That has nothing to do with our discussion.

Coming back to the topic . . .

Let's stick to the topic.

informal   You're going off on a tangent.

Asking for Brevity

→ Could you be brief?

→ Could you get to the point / spare us the details?

→ How about putting that in fewer words?

→ What are you trying to say exactly?

→ What's your point?

→ Cut to the chase.

Defusing a Situation

→ We'd better take a breather / a time-out first.

→ Maybe we should all cool off first.

→ Let's calm down / keep a level head.

→ Let's not jump off the deep end / get all wound up / get ahead of ourselves.

→ Let's not fly off the handle / get carried away.

→ Don't get your shirt / shorts in a knot.

→ Keep your shirt on!

→ Would you mind / watch your language?

→ That remark was uncalled for.

Restoring Order

→ Could we have some order please?

→ Will everyone calm down / settle down?

→ Let's not all talk at once!

→ Quiet down!

→ Silence / order, please!

In Conclusion

Whereas an informal discussion can end in a simple summary or conclusion, a more formal discussion at work or in an organization will probably end in an official decision that requires members to make a motion and to vote.

Summarizing

→ To summarize / sum up / recap . . .

→ In brief / short / summary . . .

→ To make a long story short . . .

→ Long story short . . .

→ So far . . .

→ In a nutshell . . .

Drawing Conclusions

→ To conclude our discussion, it looks like the project will come in under budget after all.

→ Therefore / thus / so we can conclude that . . .

→ It's safe to say that . . .

→ In conclusion . . .

→ All in all / all things considered . . .

→ Altogether / overall . . .

➜ Therefore / thus . . .

➜ The upshot is . . .

Last Words

➜ Would anyone like to make one last comment?

➜ Are there any last / final words on the matter?

➜ Now is the chance to make a final comment.

➜ This is your last chance.

➜ Speak now, or forever hold your peace.

➜ Any last comments?

Making a Motion

➜ I'd like to move / to make a motion that we increase our membership fees by 10 percent.

➜ I move / resolve that . . .

➜ I second the motion.

Asking for a Vote or Consensus

➜ Could we have a show of hands?

➜ Who's in favor / against?

➜ Are we all in agreement?

➜ All in favor say yes / yea.

➜ All against say no / nay.

➜ Are there any dissenters?

➜ For / against?

Wrapping Up

→ I'd like to thank the participants for their input / contributions.

→ I appreciate your input / participation / contributions.

→ Thanks for coming / being here / taking part.

→ Good job, everybody.

Ending the Discussion

formal

The meeting's adjourned until next week.

That concludes our discussion / meeting.

That wraps it up for this week / time.

That's all until next time / meeting.

That was that.

That's it, folks.

Until next time / meeting.

informal   Same time same place.

Dialogue: The Holiday Party

Underline or highlight the phrases from the chapter.

Will: Now that everyone's here, I'd like to begin by thanking all of you for being on time. As you can see from the agenda, our first topic is this year's Christmas party. Has anyone got any ideas they'd like to share?

Erin: Sure, I'd like to see us do something a little different this year.

Ken: Why, what's wrong with going to the place we always go to?

Erin: Just that. It's the same restaurant, same food, same atmosphere.

Ken: Far as I know you're the only one who doesn't like it.

Erin: Don't get me wrong. I didn't say I didn't like it.

Ken: Well, that's what I understood.

Will: Let's hear from the others, okay? Comments anyone?

Deb: I don't have any objections to trying something else. Erin, what did you have in mind?

Erin: Well, for one thing we could have the party here—

Ken: Here? In the office? What for? We're here all the time.

Will: Let Erin finish first, if you don't mind, Ken.

Erin: As I was saying, we could have the party here, have the food catered, play some games, maybe even some music.

Deb: I think games would liven things up, and we'd all have a better chance to mix than when we're stuck behind a table for a couple of hours.

Tina: I can see your point, Erin, but somebody would have to organize everything and that's a lot of extra work.

Erin: I don't mind.

Will: So, if I understand correctly, Erin, you'd like to take it on.

Erin: If it's okay with everyone else, sure.

Tina: I'd be glad to give you a hand.

Will: Before we take a vote, does anyone have any further questions or anything to add?

Ben: Actually, if I could get a word in edgewise.

Will: The floor's yours, Ben.

Ben: I've been thinking. If we had the food catered, there'd be more money for drinks, right?

Erin: I'd need an estimate on the catering, but we'd have money left over.

Tina: Will, I've got a question.

Will: Go ahead, Tina.

Tina: I don't know how well games would go over, so I was wondering if you could tell us what you're suggesting?

Erin: We don't necessarily have to play games. Maybe I could come up with a contest.

Ken: Like guess the names of Santa's reindeer?

Deb: C'mon, Ken. You don't have to be sarcastic.

Will: Okay, everyone. Let's remember it's Christmas we're talking about.

Tina: I know! Why don't we exchange presents? We wouldn't need to spend more than five to ten dollars.

Deb: Yeah, and someone can dress up like Santa Claus.

Will: Hey, now wait a minute. Don't everybody look at me!

Topics for Practice

With a group of friends or classmates, discuss:

1. the details of a trip you'd like to take on a holiday weekend;
2. how you'd like to celebrate someone's birthday, a wedding, or a special occasion;
3. how you would solve traffic problems in your city;

4. what you would do if you won the lottery as a group;

5. what changes you would like to see at school or work;

6. how you can prepare yourself for an emergency situation such as an earthquake, hurricane, or fire;

7. what steps you can take together to do something for the environment;

8. how you can raise money to support a charitable organization;

9. who you want to vote for in the next election, and what you could do to support the candidate;

10. how you can make the world a better place.

Vocabulary Notes

_____

_____

_____

_____

_____

_____

_____

_____

_____

_____

_____

_____

_____

_____

_____

_____

_____

_____

CHAPTER 9

Serious Subjects

Objectives

- to discuss complaints, demands, mistakes, causes, and consequences
- to apologize and make amends
- to express certainty and possibility

Having grown up in Rio de Janeiro, Gabriela is used to making contact with tourists from all over the world. To help finance her studies in hotel and tourism management, she worked in local restaurants and resort hotels where she put her school English to good use.

Gabriela's dream is to start up her own boutique hotel, but first she needs to acquire more experience in her chosen field and, of course, to bring her English skills up to a professional level. Already on her first day at the front desk of an international hotel, Gabriela was faced with a variety of complaints and requests from a party of foreign wedding guests. She knew enough to stay calm, cool, and collected, but she found thinking on her feet in another language stressful. In those moments when she had to pacify demanding guests, the right expressions failed her. Gabriela came away not wanting the same thing to happen to her again.

I n Chapters 7 and 8 you learned how to conduct stimulating discussions based on an exchange of opinions. Unfortunately, not all discussions can be pleasant or entertaining, and not all problems can be solved through advice or sympathy, as you learned in Chapter 5. At times you will find yourself in situations that involve broader implications and that require sensitivity and tact to resolve.

Phrases

Openers: Common Concerns

➡ **I don't know why they don't do something about** the traffic congestion in the city.

➡ **They / somebody should do something about** the cost of living.

➡ **I wish somebody would do something about** homelessness.

➡ The waste of energy is **intolerable / unacceptable**.

➡ Gang violence is **really getting to be a problem / hassle / pain**.

➡ **It's about time / high time** they built a new bridge.

➡ **Don't you just hate it** when food prices keep going up for no reason?

➡ The lack of affordable housing in this city is **my pet peeve**.

> ⓘ Who is "they"? In English "they" can refer to government or any indefinite authority that we expect to solve a problem affecting the general population.

Offering Solutions to General Problems

indirect

It'd be a big / great / considerable / major improvement / change if they built a rapid transit system.

It'd make a big difference / a world of difference if they banned pesticides.

It can't / couldn't be such a big deal / problem to create affordable housing.

Everyone would benefit from a tax break for low-income families.

One solution to climate change **is / would be** to develop alternative energy.

You can / could solve unemployment **by** creating more opportunities for small or home-based business.

All they'd have to do is lower service fees.

Here's the deal: start a public education campaign on drug abuse.

direct

It's time they finally create a pedestrian zone in the downtown core.

Levels of Language

When you have to broach a difficult subject, you can end up in a war of words, or you can try through tact and courtesy to resolve the problem to the satisfaction of all parties involved. The former ends with somebody being the loser; the latter can result in a win-win situation.

How you go about discussing delicate and serious subjects is determined first by your personal style of interacting with others, and second by the culture in which you were raised. Whereas directness is appreciated in some cultures, in others politeness and saving face are valued more. In any case, the level of language you employ plays an important role in getting your message across.

Direct vs. Indirect Language

In English choice of words is important, partly because of the absence of a familiar and unfamiliar second person pronoun. *You* is *you*, regardless of a person's age, position, or authority, and of number. To show distance or respect in the English language, you can use indirect, rather than direct, language. The following examples show how to ask someone to put out his or her cigarette.

indirect

Would you be so kind as to put out your cigarette?

Would / **do you mind** putting out your cigarette?

Would you please put out your cigarette?

Could you put out your cigarette?

It'd be nice if you put out your cigarette.

I'm sorry, but you'll have to put out your cigarette.

How about putting out your cigarette?

Please put out your cigarette.

Put out your cigarette, **will you**?

direct

Put out that cigarette **now**!

Using direct or indirect language can make a difference in situations where you have to negotiate an outcome. Look at some of the ways you can turn direct into indirect language:

Direct	Indirect
I want to have . . .	I would like to have . . .
I don't want to.	I'd really rather not / I'd prefer not to.
I don't like that.	I'd really prefer something else.
I don't know.	I'm not quite sure / I'll have to check on that.
You must / have to leave.	I suggest / recommend that you not stay much longer.

Don't use your cell phone.	I'd appreciate it if you'd refrain from using your cell phone.
Stop talking!	Would you mind not talking?
I can't.	I'm afraid it's not possible.
We have no choice.	We are forced under the circumstances to . . .
No!	Let me think about this.
That's bad.	That's not particularly good.

We can also temper meaning by adding the following words as adjectives or adverbs:

➜ a little, a little more / less

➜ somewhat / rather

➜ perhaps / maybe

➜ It might / may be

➜ particularly / terribly / really / all that much

Examples:

I find the situation **somewhat** / **rather** annoying.

➜ **Perhaps** / **maybe** you could make a few changes to the schedule.

➜ We'd appreciate it if you'd be **a little more** accommodating.

➜ I don't **really** care for this seating arrangement.

Saying "No" Nicely

A negative answer can be the simplest and perhaps the most honest one, but there are times when it may be necessary to word a refusal in milder language.

→ **I'd like to** join you, **but I really have to** be somewhere else in a few minutes.

→ **Sorry, but I don't think I can** find what you're looking for.

→ **I'm afraid I can't** take your call at this moment.

→ **I'd really rather not** go into the details if you don't mind.

→ **Thanks, but** a substitute is not what I had in mind.

Being Positive

In unpleasant and stressful situations you can easily see only the negative side of things. Although optimism in such circumstances can appear inappropriate, a talent for maintaining a positive attitude can relieve stress and relax tension.

→ I'm sure / convinced / positive that your insurance will cover the damage.

→ On the bright side / on a positive note . . .

→ Looking at the positive side . . .

→ Optimistically speaking . . .

→ To be optimistic / positive . . .

Irony, Sarcasm, and Euphemism

Depending on the tone of voice, however, indirect language can be turned into direct language. What may sound "nice" may convey quite the opposite. English speakers often use irony, sarcasm, tongue-in-cheek, and euphemisms that non-native English speakers may find difficult to interpret. Take a look at the following examples:

■ **Irony** (using words that mean the opposite with the intention of being witty or funny)

Examples:

(after three days of solid rain) Don't you just love the rain?

(about unclear directions) These directions are as clear as mud.

■ **Sarcasm** (using sharp words that mean the opposite with the intention of mocking, insulting, or wounding)

Examples:

(to a slow waiter) You really didn't have to be in such a hurry!

(to someone who hasn't called you in a long time) I was wondering if maybe you'd had your phone disconnected. You never seem to use it.

■ **Tongue-in-cheek** (saying something that one doesn't mean seriously, and indicating so with a facial expression such as a wink)

Examples:

(to someone who has a hangover) My, you look fresh and bouncy this morning!

(pretending innocence) I don't know what you're talking about.

■ **Euphemism** (using mild words for something unpleasant or offensive)

Examples:

We had a *minor disagreement* (instead of big fight).

Car thief to policeman: "But I was only *borrowing* it" (instead of stealing).

Humor in English-language cultures, particularly what is known as "black" or "gallows" humor, is based on sarcasm and irony, and sitcoms and comedy routines are full of examples. Non-native speakers will wonder what's so funny, especially when a native English speaker appears to be very serious and says something ironic, sarcastic, or euphemistic with a straight face. As a non-native speaker, you will not be expected to use language like a native speaker, but you should be aware of the signals. The more positive or pleasant a remark sounds, often the more negative the meaning.

Common Rejoinders Used Ironically or Sarcastically

→ Oh really?

→ How about that!

→ You don't say!

→ I would never have guessed!

➜ Well, I'll be!

➜ Isn't that nice / lovely / just wonderful!

➜ How kind / sweet / considerate / thoughtful / interesting!

➜ I've never been so happy / glad / pleased in all my life.

➜ Thank you very much!

Complaints and Demands

In addition to discussing personal problems, as you learned in Chapter 5, you will find yourself having to deal with problems that involve other people. Perhaps you're dissatisfied with the service you received in a store, or someone made a mistake that negatively affects you. Complaints and demands require a degree of tact and determination when you want to get your point across.

Making a Complaint

➜ **I wish to express my dissatisfaction / disappointment with / concern about** the charges on my last statement.

➜ **I want / wish to complain about / to object to** the noise in the building.

➜ **I'd like to file / to lodge a complaint** against my landlord.

➜ **There seems to be a problem with / mistake on** my invoice.

➜ **I have a complaint / beef about / an issue with** the repairs that were done to my car.

➜ **I'm upset / unhappy / dissatisfied / displeased / annoyed with** my order.

→ **I'm having a problem with** my cable service.

→ My prescription is **not okay** / **in order** / **how it should be**.

→ **Somebody messed up on** my points card.

Asking for Details

→ What exactly / specifically seems to be the matter / the problem?

→ What is the exact nature of your complaint?

→ Can you give me a detailed account of the event?

→ Can you provide us with details / specifics?

→ What's all the fuss?

Responding to a Complaint

→ I'll see what I can do about it.

→ We'll take care of / see to it right away.

→ We're here to help you.

→ I'm sure we can work this out / get to the bottom of this.

Showing Understanding or Agreement

See page 96 for phrases to show sympathy and understanding, and page 152 for agreeing with an opinion.

Misinformation

→ **I was led / made to believe that** the service was included in the price.

→ **I was under the impression that** I would receive air miles.

→ **I thought / understood that** there were no interest charges on the balance.

→ **I was told / informed that** an agent would take care of the matter.

→ **They / someone told me that** there were no extra service fees.

Stating a Request

indirect **I don't mean to trouble / bother you, but it'd be really helpful if** you could check my account.

I'd really appreciate it if / be most grateful if you checked my account.

Would it be possible for you to check my account?

Would you mind checking my account?

It would really help if you checked my account.

I was wondering if you would check my account.

Do you think you could check my account?

Can / will you check my account?

direct **Please** check my account.

▌ Making Demands

formal **I insist / demand that** you cancel the charges / the charges be cancelled.*

I have a right to / am entitled to a cancellation of the charges.

You must / have to / had better cancel the charges.

You need to cancel the charges.

I expect you to cancel the charges / the charges to be cancelled.

If you don't cancel the charges, I'll close my account.

informal Cancel the charges **or else**.

▌ Being Firm

→ That's out of the question.

→ I'm not budging / moving / giving an inch.

→ I'm sticking to my guns.

→ I insist on my rights.

→ He's playing hardball.

→ You drive a hard bargain.

---

*ⓘ The verb *to insist* is another of the few, like *to recommend* and *to suggest*, that take the subjunctive. See page 98.

Rules and Conditions

When you enter into agreements or arrangements with other people, it is necessary to state the rules and conditions in specific and detailed language so that everyone knows what is expected of him or her.

Conditions

→ **If** you sign a three-year contract, you will get a cell phone for free.

→ **Unless** you sign a three-year contract, you will have to pay extra for the cell phone.

→ You will get a free cell phone **provided / on the condition that / given that** you sign a three-year contract.

→ **As long as** you sign a three-year contract, you will get a cell phone for free.

→ **Subject to / depending on** the contract, you either will get a cell phone for free or have to pay extra for it.

→ The cost of the cell phone **depends on / is contingent upon** the length of the contract.

→ **The terms of the contract state that** you must sign a three-year contract in order to get a free cell phone.

Rules and Regulations

→ Parking is **not permitted / allowed** on this street.

→ Smoking is **prohibited / forbidden / banned** on airplanes.

→ **According to the rules / law** you may not use handheld devices while driving.

→ **The rules state / say that** you may not / you are not allowed to use a handheld device while driving.

→ Use of the pool and whirlpool **will be limited to** the hours between 10:00 a.m. and 4:00 p.m.

→ All guests and residents **will be liable for** any damage to the property.

→ **No returns on sale items**.

Importance

→ **It is important / necessary / essential to** read the terms of the agreement carefully.

→ **Especially / particularly / importantly / firstly** you should read the terms of the agreement carefully.

→ **First and foremost / above all / in particular** you should read the contract carefully.

→ **Whatever you do**, read the contract carefully.

→ This inquiry has **high priority**.

Bad News and Good News

According to a popular saying, no news is good news. Delivering good news can be a pleasant task, whereas breaking bad news is difficult, especially when you risk having to disappoint or anger another person. In both cases, you can use a variety of phrases that will fit the situation.

Bad News

→ I regret to say / to inform you that there has been an accident.

→ I hate to break this to you, but . . .

→ I'm sorry / afraid to have to say that . . .

→ I'm not sure / don't know how to tell you this, but . . .

→ It gives me no pleasure at all to tell you that . . .

→ I wish I had another way to break this to you but . . .

→ Unfortunately / regrettably / apparently . . .

→ It seems / appears that . . .

→ For some reason / some odd reason . . .

→ You may not want to hear this, but . . .

Avoiding an Unpleasant Subject

→ Do you think you could change the subject?

→ Can't we talk about / discuss this some other time?

→ Do I have to hear / listen to this?

→ I'm really not interested.

→ That's not what I need to hear right now.

→ Spare me the details.

→ Keep it to yourself!

Changing the Subject

→ If you don't mind, I'd like to change the subject / topic.

→ It would be nice if we changed the subject / topic.

→ Could / can we change the subject?

→ Can't we talk about something else?

→ Haven't we discussed / talked about this enough already?

→ How about switching to another subject / topic / something more pleasant?

Good News

→ Fortunately / luckily no one was hurt and nothing valuable was lost in the fire.

→ As luck would have it . . .

→ On the good / positive / bright side . . .

→ Lucky for you . . .

→ It turned out that . . .

→ Today's your lucky day!

Causes and Consequences

The expected result or consequence of a particular action is an important factor in any in-depth discussion. Before you can arrive at an acceptable solution, you will also want to investigate the cause of the problem.

Cause and Effect

➜ Mail delivery will be disrupted **because** / **since** / **as** there is a postal strike.

➜ Mail delivery will be disrupted **because of** / **due to** / **as a result of** / **on account of** the postal strike.

➜ There's a postal strike; **therefore** / **as a result** / **consequently** mail delivery will be disrupted.

➜ **Due to the fact that** there's a postal strike, mail delivery will be disrupted.

➜ **As long as** there's a postal strike, mail delivery will be disrupted.

Results and Consequences

➜ The postal strike can **cause** / **lead to** / **result in** / **be responsible for** a disruption in mail delivery.

➜ The disruption in mail delivery **is attributed to** / **could happen because of** / **is a direct result of** the postal strike.

➜ The postal strike could **lead to** / **result in** / **contribute to** a disruption in mail delivery.

→ **As a result of** / the **consequence of** / **due to** the postal strike, mail delivery will be disrupted.

→ **The result** / **consequence** / **outcome of** the mail strike will be a disruption in mail delivery.

→ There's a postal strike; **hence**, a disruption in mail delivery will occur.

→ **If** nothing is done about the postal strike, there will be a disruption in mail delivery.

→ The mail strike will **end up** in a disruption of mail delivery.

→ **Worst-case scenario** would be a disruption in mail delivery.

Effects

→ Social-networking **affects** / **impacts** / **influences** communication.

→ Social-networking **has an effect** / **impact** / **influence** on communication.

→ Social-networking **has made** / **makes a difference to** communication.

To express the degree of effect one thing has on another, you can add the following adjectives (and adverbs):

Positive	Negative
major / significant	minor
serious / grave	slight / minimal
permanent / lasting	temporary

Certainty and Possibility

Nobody can see the future. Nevertheless, before you make a decision or reach an agreement, you will need to predict the outcome or at least consider the possibilities.

Certainty

→ 100 percent	Our candidate **will** / **won't** win the election.
→ 99 percent	Our candidate **can't** / **couldn't** lose the election.
→ 95 percent	Our candidate **must** / **has** to win the election.
	Our candidate **can** win the election.
→ 75 to 90 percent	Our candidate **should** / **ought** / **is bound** / **is likely** to win the election.
	Chances are / **there's a (good) chance** our candidate will win the election.
→ Less than 50 percent	Our candidate **could** win the election.
	Our candidate **may** / **might** win the election.

Making Deductions About Recent Results

→ 100 percent   The CPI (consumer price index) **has increased**.

                                The CPI **couldn't have** decreased.

→ 95 percent   The CPI **has to have** / **must have** increased.

→ 75 percent   The CPI **could have** increased.

→ 50 percent   The CPI **might** / **may have** increased.

Possibility

→ **It is possible** / **feasible** / **plausible** to build a city on the moon.

→ **Someone can** / **could** build a city on the moon.

→ **There are ways to** build a city on the moon.

→ Building a city on the moon is **doable** / **viable**.

→ **It wouldn't surprise me if** someone built a city on the moon.

Impossibility

→ **It is impossible** / **unfeasible** / **implausible** / **unrealistic** / **not viable** to build a city on the moon.

→ **There's no way** / **no possible way** that people could build a city on the moon.

→ A city on the moon **couldn't / won't happen in a million years**.

→ Building a city on the moon is **ridiculous / ludicrous / a stretch / a pipe dream / an illusion / out of this world**.

To increase the degree of certainty/uncertainty or possibility/impossibility you can use the following adverbs:

→ 100 percent certainly, definitely, absolutely, unquestionably, undoubtedly

→ 80–90 percent probably, most likely, likely, surely, highly, in all likelihood

→ less than 50 percent perhaps, maybe, possibly, conceivably, for all one knows

Examples:

There will **definitely** be some big changes coming.

The government will **probably** cut social programs to save money.

For all one knows we could run out of oil sooner than we think.

Apologies and Agreements

A simple apology can be the best way to heal hurt feelings and make amends for mistakes and misunderstandings. *Sorry* may be a small word, but saying you're sorry can go a long way.

Making Apologies

formal

May I offer my sincere apologies for the inconvenience / for inconveniencing you?

Please accept my apologies for the mistake / oversight / inconvenience / trouble.

I apologize for the trouble / putting you out.

I deeply regret our error / causing you such inconvenience.

I'm terribly sorry about the mistake.

I didn't mean to offend you / step on your toes.

Sorry for your trouble.

informal **My apologies.**

Demanding an Apology

→ Your actions **call for an apology**.

→ **I expect / demand / insist on a full / complete apology**.

→ I think **I'm entitled to an apology**.

→ Any considerate person **would apologize**.

→ **I won't accept anything but a full apology**.

Expressing Regrets

→ **I shouldn't have** been so careless / **I should have** been more careful.

→ **I wish I hadn't** been so careless / **I had** been more careful.

➔ **I regret** my carelessness / having been careless / that I was careless.

➔ **Regretfully** I was careless.

➔ My carelessness was **regrettable**.

➔ **I'm sorry about** my carelessness.

Accepting an Apology

formal   I accept your apology.

            Apologies accepted.

            Don't worry / bother.

            It could have been worse.

            It's not your fault.

            No harm done.

            Never mind.

            Forget it.

informal   No problem.

Refusing an Apology

➔ An apology's a nice gesture, but I need more than that.

➔ I expect more than a mere apology.

➔ I'm sorry but it's not enough.

➔ An apology / nice words won't do it.

➔ That's just an easy way out.

Offering an Excuse

→ I'd really like to help you out, but I'm not in a position to do anything about it.

→ I'm sorry, but it's not up to me / my responsibility / my department.

→ I wish I could, but it's not in my power.

→ I didn't have anything to do with it.

→ You'll have to ask someone else.

→ There's really nothing I can do.

→ You've got the wrong person / department.

→ It must have gotten lost in the shuffle / fallen through the cracks.

→ My hands are tied.

Recognizing an Error or Accident

minor **Oops!** I dropped my pen.

Whoops! I missed the trash can.

Yikes! I spilled coffee on the new tablecloth.

Uh-oh! I left my wallet in the hotel room.

serious **Oh no / my God!** I locked the keys in the car.

Making Amends

formal **We'd be more than happy to** reimburse / compensate you for your trouble / the inconvenience.

I'm more than confident that we can come to an agreement / settlement.

I'll do my best to see that you're compensated for the trouble.

I'd like to make amends for the misunderstanding.

We'll do all we can to see this right / to clear this up.

Let me see what I can arrange / work out / do for you.

What kind of compensation can we offer you?

informal   How can we make it up to you?

Settling Differences

→ How about if we settle our differences / the score?

→ I hope there are no bad / ill feelings.

→ I'm sure we can iron this out.

→ Let's bury the hatchet.

→ Let bygones be bygones.

Making Compromises

→ We need some give and take on this.

→ Can we meet in the middle / halfway?

→ Let's split the difference.

→ We can work something out.

→ It's a win-win situation.

Coming to Agreement

→ Let's shake on it / sign on the dotted line.

→ You've got a deal.

→ You have my word.

→ We're good to go / all set.

→ We can give it the go-ahead / green light.

→ It's a deal!

→ Agreed!

Dialogue: A Hard Bargain

Underline or highlight the phrases from the chapter.

Landlord: Now, what's the nature of your complaint?

Tenant A: For three months now we've been putting up with constant noise due to repair work on the building exterior.

Landlord: I understand that some repair work was to be done on the façade and balconies, and it will certainly improve the overall appearance of the building.

Tenant A: But there's been constant banging and jackhammering for three months now.

Tenant B: And because of the extreme noise, we are frequently forced to leave the building.

Landlord: That's unfortunate, but the good news is it won't last forever.

Tenant A: Regardless we'd like to know why we were never informed before we signed our lease. If you'll remember, we clearly stated from the outset that we both work from home.

Tenant B: Under the present circumstances, the noise level could potentially impact our livelihood.

Landlord: I do apologize for the inconvenience, but there's nothing I can do about it.

Tenant A: When we agreed to rent the condo, we were led to believe that we were moving into a quiet building.

Landlord: Under normal circumstances, it is a quiet building. Perhaps you should contact the management company who is overseeing the repair work.

Tenant B: But we signed the lease with you, not them.

Landlord: Well, if you want to move out, you are free to do so.

Tenant A: And pay a penalty for breaking the lease?

Landlord: Those are the terms of the lease agreement, yes.

Tenant B: Considering that we're not at fault in all of this, I don't think that's fair at all!

Landlord: So what is it exactly that you want from me?

Tenant A: Legally we are entitled to compensation for loss of peaceful enjoyment.

Landlord: Well, for your information these repairs are costing *me* thousands of dollars, and although I'm legally entitled to raise the rent every year, I did not do so.

Tenant A: We could go to arbitration, but we'd prefer to settle with you.

Landlord: I appreciate the gesture, but it puts me on the spot. I suppose I could offer you a 10 percent reduction from now until you move out.

Tenant B: Actually I was thinking of a 30 percent rent reduction retroactively.

Landlord: I'm sorry, but that's out of the question.

Tenant A: Like we said, we could go to arbitration.

Landlord: Okay, here's the deal: I'll split the difference, but on the condition that I require one full month's notice.

Tenant A: That's understood. (*To Tenant B*) I'm okay with that if you are.

Tenant B: Well, it's not exactly win-win, but I guess it's better than nothing.

Topics for Practice

Change the following into indirect language:

1. I don't like that.

2. The service in here is terrible.

3. You made a mistake.

4. I don't understand you.

5. It's all your fault!

6. What a stupid idea!

7. I can't help you.

8. That's ridiculous.

9. I don't know!

10. What do you mean?

How would you complain about:

1. a mistake on your phone bill;
2. a package that you received by mistake;
3. having to wait a long time to get an appointment;
4. a bad mark on an unfair test paper;
5. poor service in a restaurant;
6. a heating system in your office or home that doesn't work properly;
7. having been overcharged for a car repair;
8. lost luggage at the airport;
9. rush hour traffic in your city;
10. ongoing construction noise in your office or apartment building?

Vocabulary Notes

_____

_____

_____

_____

_____

_____

_____

_____

_____

_____

_____

_____

_____

_____

_____

_____

_____

_____

_____

_____

_____

PART 3

Phrases for Special Occasions

"Good words are worth much, and cost little."

—George Herbert

CHAPTER 10

Special Occasions

Objectives

- to host informal and formal gatherings
- to extend wishes on a variety of social occasions

A s you have learned in the previous sections, there is a wide choice of phrases at your disposal for carrying on a conversation or discussion. Special occasions, such as award ceremonies, birthdays, weddings, holidays, and many more, come with special phrases that may not be on the tip of your tongue when you need them. Not knowing the right words at the right moment can be embarrassing, but you do not have to be a motivational speaker to master those little words that often mean quite a lot.

Phrases

Openers: Words of Welcome

→ Good morning / afternoon / evening, ladies and gentlemen / friends / colleagues / fellow members / guests.

→ I'd like to welcome everyone to our meeting / gathering / celebration.

→ Welcome, ladies and gentlemen / everyone.

→ Hello / hi / greetings, everyone.

→ It's good / nice / great to see all of you.

→ I'm glad you could all be here today / this evening.

Honors and Awards

When it comes to presenting and accepting awards, you can find yourself at a loss for words not only because you may be nervous but also because you want to say just the right thing.

Presenting an Award or Honor

→ It gives me great pleasure to call upon Elena to accept this award / scholarship / trophy.

→ And the award / scholarship / trophy goes to Yuan-Ting.

→ We're gathered here to pay tribute to a great friend and colleague.

→ Please stand up for / put your hands together for Ali.

→ And now, the moment we've all been waiting for.

Acceptance Speeches

→ I'm honored / pleased / thrilled to accept this award / scholarship / trophy.

→ It's a great honor / pleasure for me to accept this award.

→ I'd like to thank / to express my gratitude to my parents / family / wife / husband / partners / teachers.

→ I couldn't have done it without the support of my parents / family ...

→ My speech would not be complete without a word of thanks to ...

→ My heartfelt thanks / deepest appreciation goes out to ...

Announcements

→ Ladies and gentlemen, I'm pleased to announce / report that this year has been a very successful one.

→ I'd like to take this opportunity to announce the winners of the competition.

→ I want to make a special announcement at this time.

→ If you would lend me your ear for this short announcement.

→ Could I have everyone's attention?

A Job Well Done

→ I'd just like to thank everyone for their efforts / a job well done / pitching in.

→ I want everyone to know how much I appreciate your efforts.

→ Your team effort has made success possible.

→ You've all done a great job.

→ Way to go, team!

Congratulations

→ Congratulations on your graduation / promotion / the birth of your child.

→ I'd like to congratulate you on . . .

→ All the best for your studies / new job / family!

→ We're really proud of you!

→ Good show!

→ Lots of luck!

Special Occasions

One look in the greeting-card section of any gift shop or drugstore will show you the number of occasions there are to celebrate. Whereas a greeting card may express what you mean to say more poetically and even cleverly, the most sincere wishes are those you deliver yourself in simple, personal, and heartfelt language.

Toasts

→ Let's drink / raise a glass to the bride and groom.

→ Here's a toast to the happy couple / the graduates.

→ Here's to you!

Birthdays

→ We wish you a happy birthday!

→ All the best on your birthday!

→ Best wishes on your birthday!

→ Many happy returns!

→ Happy Birthday!

→ May all your wishes come true!

Weddings and Engagements

→ Congratulations on your engagement / wedding!

→ We wish you a long and happy marriage / life together.

→ All the best for the future.

→ Our blessings to you!

→ You make a lovely couple!

Anniversaries

→ Happy Anniversary!

→ May you have many more years together!

Giving a Present

→ Please accept this present as a token of our appreciation / affection.

→ Here's a little something for you.

→ This is for you.

Accepting a Present

➜ That's very thoughtful / considerate of you.

➜ You really shouldn't have.

➜ You didn't have to.

➜ You're too much!

➜ I can't wait to open it.

➜ How sweet!

➜ For me?

Vacations, Holidays, and Trips

Although it may not be necessary to wish someone a good trip or a nice weekend, it's common courtesy to do so.

Wishes for the Weekend, Holidays, and Vacation

➜ Have a good / great weekend / holiday / vacation.

➜ Have a good time / fun on your holiday / vacation.

➜ I hope you have a great holiday / weekend / vacation.

➜ Enjoy your vacation.

➜ Have a great / safe trip / flight / journey.

➜ Bon voyage!

Welcoming Someone Back

➜ It's good to see you're back.

➜ Great / nice / good to have you back.

→ We're glad you're back.

→ We missed you.

→ Welcome back.

National Holidays

→ Christmas	Merry Christmas / Happy Christmas / Season's Greetings!
→ New Year's	Happy New Year!
→ Easter	Happy Easter!
→ Thanksgiving	Happy Thanksgiving!
→ General	Happy Holidays!

Dining

Anyone would agree that a celebration or social occasion in any culture wouldn't be the same without food and drink.

Toasts

→ Here's to your health.

→ Let's drink to your health.

→ Here's looking at you!

→ Cheers!

→ Bottoms up!

Before a Meal

(i) Although you can use the following expressions to wish someone a good meal or "appetite" before a meal, there is no authentic expression in English, and so English has borrowed from French. In fact, people in English-speaking countries rarely say anything before a meal. Why? That's a good question to which this author hasn't found a good answer.

On the other hand, it is more common, particularly among Christian families in the United States, to say "grace" before a meal; that is, to thank God or ask Him to bless the food. While grace is being said, people at the table bow their heads in prayer and sometimes join hands.

➔ Bon appétit!

➔ Enjoy your meal!

➔ Have a nice meal / good lunch!

Complimenting the Host

➔ That was some / a great meal!

➔ I really enjoyed the meal!

➔ You're a great / terrific cook!

➔ The food was really delicious!

➔ You went all out / really knocked yourself out!

Relationships

Immediate Family:

→ parents   father (Dad, Daddy, Papa, Pops), mother (Mom, Mommy, Mum, Mama)

→ children   son, daughter

→ siblings   brother, sister

Relatives on your Mother's and Father's Side:

→ grandparents   grandmother (Grandma, Granny, Nana), grandfather (Grandpa, Poppa)

→ grandchildren   grandson, granddaughter

→ parents' siblings   aunt, uncle

→ children of aunt and uncle   cousins

→ children of brothers and sisters   nieces, nephew

ⓘ The addition of **great** or **great-great** indicates previous generations.

Example:

My grandmother's mother is my **great-grandmother**, and she died before I was born.

Relatives Through Marriage

→ in-laws   mother-in-law, father-in-law,
                                sister-in-law, brother-in-law

(i) If a parent remarries, you refer to the spouse as your
stepfather or stepmother, and the children as step-sisters and
step-brothers.

Example:
My **step-sister** is the same age as I am.

Marital Status:

→ single, unmarried   bachelor (male), spinster (female)

→ married, spouse   husband (male), wife (female)

→ common-law partner

→ separated, divorced

→ widowed   widower (male), widow (female)

Romance

In a well-known song, Jim Croce sings, "Every time I tried to tell
you, the words just came out wrong, so I guess I'll have to say
I love you in a song." Though it's more romantic to express our
feelings with music, we still need words.

Love and Affection

→ I **love** / **adore** you.

→ I'm **mad** / **crazy about** Marin.

→ Siobhan **thinks a lot of** / **the world of** her sister.

→ Vito and Carla are **head over heels in love**.

→ Ivan's **fallen for** Katerina **hook, line and sinker**!

→ Jeppe's **got it bad** / **the hots for** Sara.

Terms of Endearment

It's very common to call a spouse, partner, boy- or girlfriend, child or grandchild by the following terms of endearment, or pet names (not to be confused with names for a pet dog or cat).

→ angel

→ baby, babe

→ darling

→ dear, dearie

→ honey, hon'

→ love

→ sugar

→ sweetheart, sweetie

Proposing Marriage

Nowadays it's considered old-fashioned for a man to get down on one knee to propose to a woman, but the words remain the same.

→ I'm asking you for your hand in marriage.

→ Will you marry me / be my wife?

→ Let's get married / hitched!

→ Why don't we get married!

Personal Notes

Undoubedtly you have family, friends, classmates, colleagues, and acquaintances who mean a lot to you, and on an every-day basis you can show them that you care by simply saying something kind and thoughtful. As with giving presents, it's the thought that counts.

Passing on Greetings

→ Say hello / hi to your wife / husband / family for me.

→ Give my regards / best wishes to your parents.

→ Pass on my best wishes to your sister.

→ Remember me to Lasse.

Sickness

(i) Saying "Bless you" after someone sneezes is probably one of the first expressions to do with health that a non-native English speaker learns.

→ I hope you recover / get better soon.

→ Take good care of yourself.

→ Get well / better soon!

Condolences in the Case of Death

→ I'm sorry for your loss.

→ My sympathies / heartfelt condolences.

→ Our thoughts / prayers are with you.

→ My heart goes out to you.

→ You'll be in our prayers.

Expressing Emotions

Happiness and Joy

→ I'm over the moon / on cloud nine / on top of the world!

→ Kamal's overjoyed / elated / tickled pink!

→ Donna's thrilled / thrilled to bits / to pieces / to death!

→ I could cry / jump for joy!

→ We couldn't be happier!

→ Piotr's a happy camper / happy as a clam!

Surprise

➔ A birthday party is the last thing I was expecting!

➔ You don't mean to say / to tell me you're going to be a grandmother!

➔ Your invitation caught me by surprise!

➔ I'm speechless / dumbstruck / at a loss for words.

➔ I don't know what to say!

➔ You've got to be kidding!

➔ Who'd have guessed!

➔ You don't say!

➔ Don't tell me!

➔ Holy cow / smokes / Toledo!

➔ Oh my God!

Dialogue: Happy Birthday!

Underline or highlight the phrases from the chapter.

Andy: Okay, everybody. Here she comes. (*He turns off light.*)

Ella: (*She opens the door.*) Hey, why's it so dark in here? (*She turns on the light.*)

Together: Surprise! Surprise!

Ella: What—

Together: Happy Birthday, Ella!

Ella: Oh, my goodness!

Maya: Many happy returns!

Andy: Happy Birthday, honey!

Dave: All the best, Ella!

Ella: I don't believe it!

Dave: And here comes Maya with the birthday cake. (*Everyone sings "Happy Birthday."*)

Ella: My, you shouldn't have gone to such trouble.

Andy: Well, you only turn 40 once.

Ella: I was hoping you'd all forget.

Dave: Think of it this way, Ella: you're not getting older, you're getting better.

Ella: Isn't that what they say on hair color commercials?

Maya: Come on, Ella, blow out the candles, and don't forget to make a wish.

Ella: Okay, I won't. Here goes. (*She blows out the candles.*)

Andy: Good job! Now time for a toast! (*He hands out glasses of champagne.*) Here's to Ella!

Dave: To your health and happiness!

Maya: And to many more birthdays!

Ella: Cheers!

(*Everyone drinks.*)

Ella: Wow, my favorite champagne! This can't get any better.

Andy: Wait till you open this.

Ella: You didn't! I don't know what to say.

Andy: Don't say anything. Just open it.

Ella: (*She opens the envelope.*) A spa certificate! I don't believe it! Honestly, this makes my day.

Maya: And here's a little something from us to go with it.

Ella: A bathrobe! You guys are too much. Thanks. (*She gives everyone a hug and kiss.*)

Andy: So, what do you say we go out for dinner and celebrate in style?

Ella: What about the cake?

Andy: We can save it for later.

Dave: So, what are we waiting for?

Maya: Ella, I know you're not supposed to tell, but what did you wish for?

Ella: To be 39 again.

Vocabulary Notes

_____

_____

_____

_____

_____

_____

_____

_____

_____

_____

_____

_____

_____

_____

_____

_____

_____

_____

_____

_____

_____

_____

PART 4

Phrases for Telephone and Video Conversations

"The telephone is a good way to talk to people without having to offer them a drink."

—Fran Lebowitz

CHAPTER 11

Telephone Basics

Objectives

- to initiate and end a basic telephone call
- to perform simple tasks on the telephone

When Thao and Duong Tran immigrated to America, they dreamed of starting up their own Vietnamese restaurant. Running a restaurant, however, will require them to conduct much of their business over the telephone, and Thao feels somewhat intimidated by the prospect of dealing with people she cannot see. Will she know what to say? And what if the person she's dealing with

doesn't understand her? Or she doesn't understand them? How will she get the services or supplies she needs?

Now that the telephone has developed from rotary dial to cellular and smart phones, with almost as many mobile phone subscribers as there are people on Earth, the telephone has become indispensable to personal as well as business communication.

In terms of content, telephone conversations do not differ greatly from face-to-face conversations. There are, however, specific phrases used in telephone calls, particularly in formal business situations. What you say and how you say it are important not only in making a good impression, but in getting your message across.

Phrases

Making a Call

In English-speaking cultures, it is customary for people to identify themselves on the telephone with their first and last names. Very rarely do people refer to themselves as Mr., Mrs., Ms., and so on. (See Introducing Yourself, page 9.)

In a formal business situation, you should state both your name and the name of your company, organization, or department. If you are unknown to the person whom you are calling, it's a good idea to give your last name as well.

Identifying Yourself as the Caller

→ Good morning / good afternoon, **this is** Mary O'Reilly from Summit Publishing.

→ Hello, **my name is** Steven Nugent.

→ Hi, **it's** Kim.

If you're calling for someone else, you can say:

→ Hello, I'm **calling on behalf of** Adam at Brightman Securities.

Asking to Speak to Someone

→ **I'd like to speak to** Margaret Burke.

→ **Could / may I speak to / with** Bill?

→ **Would you put me through to** an agent / a salesperson?

→ **Can I talk to someone** in the insurance department?

→ **Is** Brenda **in / there**?

Stating the Reason for Calling

→ **I'm calling about / concerning / regarding / in regard to** a loan application.

→ **The reason I'm calling is to** inquire about your rates / make a complaint.

→ **I just wanted to** touch base / reach out.

Checking to See Who's Answering

In case you're not sure if you've reached the right person, particularly if the person on the other end hasn't identified him- or herself, you will need to verify. Also, when you receive a call, there may be times when you don't understand or catch the caller's name.

➜ **To / with whom** am I speaking again?

➜ **Am I speaking to** Customer Service?

➜ **Is this** Jane / the Ferguson residence?

Asking for an English Speaker

➜ I'd like to talk to an English speaker.

➜ Is there someone there who speaks English?

➜ Do you speak English?

Receiving a Call

When answering the phone in a more formal or business situation, you should give information in the following order:

- ■ company, department or office name, and greeting
- ■ speaker's name
- ■ offer to help

Stating the company phone number is another, but rather uncommon, way to answer the phone. In an informal situation, such as at home, you can answer simply with "Hello."

Some people may answer with "Smith residence," for example, although this is outdated.

And remember, it's always a good idea to put a smile in your voice that will make you sound friendly and helpful to the caller.

Giving the Company, Department, or Office Name and Greeting

→ Good morning / good afternoon, Summit Publishing.

→ Hello, Customer Service.

→ Thank you for calling Brewster and Wyman.

Giving the Speaker's Name

→ **This is** Erin Maguire.

→ Sean **speaking**.

→ Marjorie **here**.

Offering to Help

→ How may / can I direct your call?

→ How may / can I help / assist you?

→ Can I be of assistance?

→ What can I do for you today?

All three components together will sound like this:

- Good morning, Summit Publishing. Erin speaking. How may I direct your call?

- Thank you for calling Brewster and Wyman. How can I be of assistance?

- Hello. Service Center. Sean speaking. What can I do for you?

Confirming Yourself as the Person Answering a Call

When you answer the phone and the caller asks to speak to you, you can reply:

➜ This is she / he.

➜ Speaking.

Asking Why the Person Is Calling

➜ May I ask what you're calling about / in regard to / in reference to?

➜ What is the nature of your call?

➜ And what is the call about / regarding / concerning?

Checking Details

When speaking on the phone, you may misunderstand or miss information for a variety of reasons: background noise, a bad connection, a person's accent, or your own nervousness.

Checking to See Who's Calling

➜ May I ask who's calling?

➜ What was your name again?

➜ And your name, please?

Interrupting

➜ Excuse me, you were saying?

➜ Just a minute, I don't think I got / understood / caught that.

→ Sorry, I didn't catch that.

→ I beg your pardon.

→ Pardon me.

→ Come again.

A Bad Connection

→ I'm sorry, we seem to have a bad connection.

→ There's something wrong with this line.

→ Are you still there / on the line?

→ Hello?

Asking the Person to Repeat Details

→ I'm sorry to interrupt, but could you speak more slowly / repeat that?

→ I'm afraid I'm having trouble understanding.

→ Would you repeat that more slowly this time?

→ You were saying?

Connecting a Call

At work or at home, there are occasions when you will reach some-one—a secretary, receptionist, or relative—other than the person with whom you want to speak. If it's a secretary or receptionist, that person should automatically connect you or "put you through," or "put you on hold" until the person is available. Depending on the nature of the call and your success, or lack of success, in getting what you want, you can ask to be connected with someone else.

Putting a Call Through

→ Just a moment, please. I'll put you through.

→ Just a minute. I'll connect / transfer your call to Customer Care.

→ Hold the line, please and I'll see if Bill's available / free / in.

→ Let me transfer your call to an account manager.

→ Hold on / hang on a sec'. I'll get her.

Announcing a Caller

→ I have Veronica Gutierrez on the line.

→ I have a call for you from a Thomas Straub.

→ Bradley Jones is asking to speak to you.

→ It's your son.

Putting a Caller on Hold

→ I'm sorry, Michel's on another line. **Would you like to hold?**

→ Dr. Lennon'll be a couple of minutes. **Can I put you on hold?**

→ **Do you mind holding / waiting** while I pull up your information?

→ **Is it all right if I put you on hold** while I check your account?

→ I'm sorry to interrupt, but **can you hold** while I take another call?

→ Just hang on.

Reconnecting after Putting a Caller on Hold

→ Hello, I have Michel on the line now.

→ Hello, I'll put you through now.

→ Beth, are you still there?

Information and Services

Telephone calls are the most common way to obtain information easily and quickly.

Asking for Information

→ **I'm calling to inquire about / ask about** your hours of operation.

→ **I'd like to have** the extension for Ms. Puccini's office.

→ **Would you give me** Jorge's cell phone number, please?

→ **I was wondering if you could send** me your latest catalog.

→ **Can you provide me with** an updated price list?

→ **I need some information about** travel insurance.

→ **What can you tell me** about the apartment for rent?

Emergency Calls

In case of emergency, **911** is the number to call in North America, whereas **112** is widely used internationally. You will be required to give the dispatcher (person who takes your call) the following information:

- your name, location, and phone number
- the nature of the emergency: illness, accident, threat to your safety such as fire or break-in.

What You Will Hear

→ 911, what's your emergency?

→ Emergency, how can I help?

→ What's the nature of your call?

→ Can you tell me what happened?

→ Is anyone hurt / wounded / injured / unconscious / in immediate danger?

Asking for Help

→ Please send an ambulance as soon as possible / right away!

→ I need immediate / urgent assistance.

→ This is an emergency!

→ Please help me!

Expressing Urgency

→ This is urgent / important / critical!

→ It can't wait!

→ I'm in danger!

→ Please hurry!

(See additional emergency phrases, page 125.)

Asking about Wait Times

→ How long will it take?

→ How soon will the ambulance / doctor / firetruck arrive?

→ Will it take very long?

Describing a Victim

→ He can't breathe / is having difficulty breathing.

→ I'm bleeding / in terrible pain.

→ She's not breathing / not moving / not responding to anything.

→ He's unconscious / not alert.

→ He's vomiting / throwing up.

Reporting Danger

→ **I'm calling to report** an accident / a break-in / a fire.

→ **There's been** an accident at the corner of 4th Street and Broadway Avenue.

➔ **There's something** strange / unusual / suspicious going on across the street.

➔ **Someone is trying to** break into my house.

➔ **There's** smoke coming from the kitchen.

Telephone Etiquette

In business situations, it is important to use polite formal language on the telephone.

(See Direct vs. Indirect Language, page 202.)

Saying "Please"

➔ **Would it be possible to** speak to the manager?

➔ **I'd appreciate it if** you'd put me through right away.

➔ If it's not any / too much trouble / bother.

➔ If you don't / wouldn't mind.

Expressing Thanks

➔ **I appreciate** it / that / your help!

➔ **I'm very grateful for** your assistance.

➔ **I'd like to thank you for** your efforts.

➔ **Thank you** very much / a lot for your call / returning my call.

➔ **Thanks** a lot!

Response

Remember that "Please" is not a response to "thank you." When someone thanks you for something, it is customary to reply with:

→ You're welcome! (more common in North America than in Great Britain)

→ My pleasure / The pleasure was all mine!

→ Don't mention it!

→ Not at all!

→ No problem!

(☐ See Appreciation and Gratitude, page 103.)

Calling a Wrong Number

Because people move and forget to change their contact information, or they press the wrong digits when dialing, they can end up reaching you by mistake. Or for the same reasons, you might reach the wrong person.

→ I'm sorry, I must have the wrong number.

→ I seem to have the wrong number.

Receiving a Call to the Wrong Number

→ You've got / must have the wrong number.

→ There's no one here by that name.

Unwanted Calls

Unless you have an unlisted number (a number that doesn't appear in a telephone book), there will be times when you receive annoying calls from telemarketers, poll takers, solicitors for donations, and scam artists.

→ I'm sorry, but I'm not interested.

→ Please remove my number from your records.

→ Don't call this number again.

Ending a Call

In addition to saying good-bye, as you would after any ordinary conversation, you can show your appreciation for the call or the person's assistance.

→ It was nice / good / a pleasure talking to you.

→ I look forward to your next call / to talking to you again.

→ I appreciate your call / your assistance / the information.

→ Thank you for calling. Is there anything else I can help you with?

→ Thanks for your call.

→ Good-bye.

→ Bye now.

→ Talk to you later / then.

→ Take care now.

→ See you!

Making Small Talk

When people are busy, you don't want to waste time with irrelevant or meaningless chitchat. But sometimes, starting a conversation by asking how the person is and making a comment about the weather, a recent meeting or business trip, a sports event, or work can open up the lines of communication. And it is always thoughtful to show interest in what the other person's saying. Some useful phrases are:

- Asking About Someone's Well-Being, page 23.
- Rejoinders, page 47.
- Showing Interest, page 8.

Dialogue: Touching Base

A: Good morning, Mountain Trekking. Jody speaking. How may I direct your call?

B: Hello, this is Tom Smith. I'd like to speak to Marcia Grant.

A: Oh, I'm sorry, Marcia's on another line. May I ask what you're calling about?

B: Well, I just wanted to touch base.

A: I see her line's still busy. Can I put you on hold?

B: Well, all right, if it's not too long.

A: It shouldn't be more than a minute.

(a minute later)

Marcia, I have Tom Smith on the line.

C: Go ahead, Jody. Put him through. Hi, Tom?

B: Hello, Marcia. How's it going?

C: Oh, things are pretty crazy as usual around here, but I can't complain. What's up with you?

B: Well, I've been on holiday for a couple of weeks.

C: Really? Where?

B: I was doing some skiing up at Whistler.

C: Whistler? Lucky you! I bet you had a great time.

B: I did, but now it's back to work.

C: So what can I do for you?

B: Actually, if you've got some time, I was just calling to touch base. It's been a while.

C: You aren't kidding. Time just seems to fly. Listen, Tom, I've got a meeting in half an hour to prepare for, so why don't I call you back?

B: Better yet, are you doing anything for lunch tomorrow?

C: As a matter of fact, I'm free.

B: Great, so how about I meet you at Las Palapas? Say, 12:30. My treat.

C: Sure, sounds good.

B: Okay, meet you there.

C: All right. And thanks for the invitation.

B: My pleasure. See you then.

C: Okay, bye now.

Practice

Respond to the following:

1. Thanks for calling.
2. I'd like to speak to Manuela.
3. Can I put you on hold?
4. I'm sorry, Ariel's on another line.
5. How can I direct your call?
6. May I ask who's speaking?
7. Talk to you later.
8. I'm calling to inquire about your yoga classes.
9. I have a Susan Kellerman on the line.
10. Is this [your name]?

Vocabulary Notes

_____

_____

_____

_____

_____

_____

_____

_____

_____

_____

_____

_____

_____

_____

_____

_____

_____

_____

_____

CHAPTER 12

Telephone Messages

Objectives

- take and leave messages
- state and confirm important details

I n today's busy world, it can be difficult to reach people at your convenience. Therefore, you rely on messages to communicate important information. Knowing specific phrases and observing basic message etiquette can ensure that your message is received as well as understood.

- Be brief and get to the point. Try to limit your message to 15 seconds. If necessary, prepare yourself ahead of making the call so that you know exactly what to say.

■ Speak clearly and slowly, especially when giving important details, such as phone and account numbers, or repeat them so that the person receiving your message doesn't have to replay your message several times.

Phrases

Giving Details over the Phone

Telephone messages contain important information that must be clearly stated so that the person on the receiving end knows exactly whom to contact and how to get in touch.

■ Numbers

North American phone numbers contain ten digits: for example, 604-659-3773. The first three are the area code, with the last seven belonging to an individual residence or office. When making an international call, you need to include the particular country code.

Companies and organizations have what are called 1-800, or toll-free numbers, that you can call without having to pay long-distance charges.

When giving someone a phone number, say the numbers individually (6-0-4-3-5-6-8-2-1-4) or the last four in pairs (6-0-4-3-5-6-82-14).

For repeated numbers, like 33, one can say double-three (or thirty-three); for 888, triple-eight.

The number 0 is read as zero or the letter O. With phone numbers, it doesn't matter which one you use, but if you're stating a postal code consisting of numbers and letters, it is necessary to differentiate between the two. For example, V0R, is read as V-zero-R, and 1O5 as 1-oh-5.

When giving an international number, you should state the country and city codes and phone number in a manner that is easy to write down or record as well as to understand. For example, 49 911/55 29 16: forty-nine, nine-one-one, fifty-five, twenty-nine, sixteen.

Account numbers are usually given number by number. In the case of a long account number, you should speak slowly or, if you are taking down someone's account number, repeat each number as the caller gives it.

Addresses

When giving someone an address over the phone, you can break the numbers into groups of ones and tens, rather than saying them as a complete number.

Examples:

- 683 Hollywood Crescent: six, eighty-three Hollywood Crescent (rather than six-hundred-and-eighty-three)

- 1142 Rose Street: eleven, forty-two Rose Street

- 426 964 Heywood Avenue: suite / apartment / unit number four, twenty-six, nine, sixty-four Heywood Avenue

Spelling

Because similar sounding or rhyming letters, such as *F* and *S*, or *D* and *T*, can be misunderstood over the phone, you can use the *International Telecommunications Union Standard Phonetic Alphabet* when you spell out a name or word.

Example:

Harper: H for Hotel, A for Alpha, R for Romeo, P for Papa, E for Echo, R for Romeo

A — Alpha	J — Juliet	S — Sierra
B — Bravo	K— Kilo	T — Tango
C — Charlie	L — Lima	U — Uniform
D — Delta	M — Mike	V — Victor
E — Echo	N — November	W— Whisky
F — Foxtrot	O — Oscar	X — X-ray
G — Golf	P — Papa	Y — Yankee
H — Hotel	Q — Quebec	Z — Zulu
I — India	R — Romeo	

Leaving a Message

A telephone message should include:

- your name and company or department
- the time and date of your call
- your reason for calling
- your phone number and other contact information, such as an e-mail address, and your location (e.g., a hotel room number) if you're traveling

Asking Someone to Take a Message

→ Would you give Sandor a message?

→ Would you have Olga call / ring me back?

→ Could you take a message for Helga?

→ Could you tell Martine that I'll be a few minutes late?

→ Please tell her I'm tied up in traffic.

Stating Importance

→ It's urgent / of utmost importance.

→ It's an emergency situation.

→ I need to get this information to him right away.

→ We're on a tight schedule.

→ It can't wait.

Taking a Message

When you take a message for a colleague or friend over the phone, you need to let the caller know why the person to whom they wish to speak is unavailable. You also need to ask:

■ what the call's about

■ what specific information the caller wants to pass on

When the caller gives you a number or spells a name, you should repeat the information to assure the caller that you have taken it down correctly.

Stating Unavailability

→ **I'm sorry, but** John's not available / free at the moment.

→ **I'm afraid** Frieda won't be in until tomorrow morning.

→ Marin's tied up / out of town at the moment.

Asking to Take a Message

→ Would you like me to give him a message?

→ If you'll give me your name and number, I'll have someone call you back / return your call.

→ Can / shall I take a message?

→ Is there something I can pass on to her?

Giving Assurance

When you take a message, it's important to let the caller know that his message will be passed on. Note the use of the future with "will."

→ I'll give him your message.

→ I'll pass that on to her.

→ I'll see to it right away.

→ I'll let him know as soon as he gets back.

→ I'll have her call you back / return your call right away / as soon as possible.

→ I'll see what I can do.

→ I'll do my best.

→ Will do.

▌Declining to Leave a Message

If you're calling about a personal matter or it may be difficult for someone to reach you, you can decline to leave a message.

→ Thanks, but I'll call / check back later.

→ I'd prefer to try again another time.

→ I'll try later.

▌Offering Additional Help

→ Do you need anything else / further help?

→ Is there anything else I can help you with today?

Ensuring Communication

When words fail you in a face-to-face conversation, gestures come to the rescue. Not so during telephone calls, where you need to let the person on the other end know that you're listening and that you understand him or her. In this case, a few little words can make a big difference.

→ Yes.

→ Right.

→ Okay.

→ I see / understand.

→ Go on.

(☐ For more phrases, see Discourse Markers, page 30.)

Asking for Clarification

→ Would / do you mind repeating that / going over that once more?

→ Could you walk me through that again?

→ Could you repeat that, please?

→ Can you confirm / double-check / go over my directions?

→ I'm sorry, I didn't catch your name.

→ I'm sorry, what was your name again?

→ Let me see if I've got that right.

Confirming Details

→ I'll repeat your e-mail address to verify it.

→ I'll read that back to you.

→ Let me see if I've got that right.

→ Got it!

Asking for Additional Contact Information

→ Does Eriko have your cell phone number / e-mail address?

→ Can we reach you at another number?

→ How can James get ahold of you in case there's a change in schedule?

→ Is there anyone else we can call if there's a problem?

Returning a Call

When you've received a message, the next step is to call back as soon as possible.

→ **I'm calling in response to** the message you left for me this morning.

→ Hello, **I'm following up on** your message of July 10th at 9:05.

→ This is Silvia calling back / returning your call.

→ Hello, this is Jack. You called?

→ Hi, I got your message.

Answering Machines, Voice Mail, and Text Messages

A busy schedule doesn't always allow you to leave or take messages in person, in which case technology comes in handy. When you're recording a message on a private answering machine or voice mail, it's not a good idea to let strangers know that you're away from home. The following are examples only.

Private Recordings

■ You've reached 248-5792. Please leave a message after the tone / beep.

■ Hello, this is Carly. Sorry, but I can't make it to the phone right now. Please leave a message and I'll get back to you as soon as possible.

Business Recordings

- Hello, this is Mary Sullivan's voice mail. Please be advised that I'll be out of the office until next Monday morning. If you leave a message, I'll get back to you as soon as I can. Thank you.

- You've reached the desk of Won-Ho Park. At the moment I'm either busy with a customer or at a meeting, so if you'd leave your name, time and date of call, your phone number and a short message, I'll get in touch as soon as possible. Thanks for calling and have a nice day.

Text Messages

Usually you rely on secretaries, receptionists, office colleagues, and relatives to deliver messages, but nowadays wireless technology has popularized the use of text messages. Texting has evolved into a language of its own that can be very useful, but remember that these abbreviations do not take the place of grammatical English.

ASAP	as soon as possible
ATB	all the best
ATM	at the moment
B4N	before now
BBS	be back soon
BFN/B4N	bye for now
BRT	be right there
CM	call me

CU	see you
DK	don't know
FAQ	frequently asked questions
FYI	for your information
HAND	have a nice day
IC	I see
IDK	I don't know
IMO	in my opinion
KIT	keep in touch
L8R	later
NRN	no reply necessary
PCM	please call me
PLMK	please let me know
SRY	sorry
T2Go	time to go
T2UL	talk to you later
THX	thanks
WRT	with respect to

Dialogue: A Message

A: Good morning, Picture Perfect Printing. Nikki speaking. How may I direct your call?

B: Good morning, I'd like to speak to Jack.

A: I'm sorry but he's in a meeting with a client right now. Can I take a message?

B: Yes, would you have him call Michelle back as soon as possible? My number's 250-653-8225 and he can reach me until 1:30.

A: Is there another number he can call in case he gets held up?

B: Yes, he can get me on my cell phone. It's 703-295-8840.

A: Okay, let me read those numbers back to you. 250-653-8225 and 703-295-8840.

B: That's correct.

A: And may I ask what you're calling about?

B: Yes, I have another project I'd like to discuss with him.

A: Okay, got it! I'll have him get back to you.

B: Thanks. Good-bye.

A: Good-bye and thanks for calling Picture Perfect Printing.

(later)

B: Hello.

C: Hello, Michelle? It's Jack from Picture Perfect Printing. I just got your message. So what can I do for you?

Practice

Use the information in the dialogue and fill out the message form.

WHILE YOU WERE OUT

To: _____

Date _____ **Time** _____ **A.M.** ❏ **P.M.** ❏

From: _____

Contact #: _____

❏ **called**   ❏ **wants to see you**   ❏ **came to see you**

Message: _____

_____

_____

Vocabulary Notes

_____

_____

_____

_____

_____

_____

_____

_____

_____

_____

_____

_____

_____

_____

_____

_____

_____

_____

_____

CHAPTER 13

Telephone Business

Objectives

- to make appointments, bookings, and reservations
- to place orders
- to report and discuss problems

"I could live without the internal combustion engine, MTV, and the Cuisinart. But not without the telephone," wrote Michael Levine, American writer and public relations expert. Indeed, without the telephone, most people would find it extremely difficult, if not impossible to conduct everyday business, such as setting up appointments, reporting an accident or emergency, or even ordering a pizza.

Phrases

Making Appointments

Whether it's an appointment to see your doctor, dentist, hair-dresser, or financial advisor or to set up a meeting, conference, or presentation, you can use the same basic phrases on the telephone.

Asking for an Appointment

When making an appointment, you need to give the following details:

- what the appointment is **for**, or what you need **to do**
- who the appointment is **with**, or who you want **to see**
- when the appointment is **for**

→ I'm calling **to make / set up an appointment for** a haircut / a checkup / an interview.

→ I'd like **to make an appointment with** Dr. Martin / a Member Service Representative.

→ Could you **set up an appointment to see** an insurance agent?

→ I need to **make an appointment for** next Tuesday / three o'clock.

→ When / how soon can you **get me in for** a haircut?

→ I need **to see Marion about** some urgent business.

Stating the Date

There are two ways to state the date:

- February the second
- the second of February

When giving the date, use ordinal numbers (first, second, third, fourth, fifth, etc.).

Remember: first, second, third, twenty-first, thirty-second, fifty-third, but the eleventh, twelfth, and thirteenth.

Stating the Time

- When giving the time, we use a.m. (ante-meridian) for the period between midnight and noon, and p.m. (post-meridian) for the period between noon and midnight. For example, 9:00 a.m. is in the morning and 9:00 p.m. is in the evening. Another way to avoid confusion is to say nine in the morning or six in the evening. If you're talking about a 2:00 meeting, it should be obvious that you're not scheduling it in the middle of the night.

- In North America, time expressions such as 1400 (fourteen hundred hours) appear on schedules or timetables, but are almost never used in conversation.

- When making transcontinental or international calls, you need to take time zones into account: for example, 6:00 p.m. Eastern time or 8:00 in the morning your time.

(See Time Expressions, pages 34, 131.)

Asking for the Time of the Appointment

→ When / what time would you like to come in?

→ What day / time would work for you / suit you?

→ What would be the best / most convenient time?

→ What time shall I put you down for?

→ Would 10:00 tomorrow work for you?

→ What's a good time / day for you?

→ How about Tuesday morning at 8:30?

Setting a Time as the Caller

→ Is anything available / free in the late afternoon?

→ Do you have an opening Friday morning?

→ What's the earliest available opening?

→ How soon can you get me in?

→ How about 4:00?

Checking Availability

→ Let me check / see / take a look at the schedule.

→ Just a second, I'll see what's available / free.

→ I'll see / check when there's an opening.

Confirming the Time and Date

→ 3:00 on October the 27th is not a problem.

→ 10:00 on Monday morning it is!

→ 1:00 sounds good / great / fine.

→ That'll be 4:00 on Tuesday.

→ We'll see you then.

Suggesting an Alternative Time

→ I'm sorry, Asha's booked up all morning. May I suggest the afternoon?

→ I can try and get you in to see Jochen's assistant, if that works for you.

→ Would you rather come in early?

→ How about 9:00 instead?

Making Bookings and Reservations

The phrases you use to book a flight or to make a reservation differ only in detail from those you would use to make an appointment.

→ I'd like to book / reserve a double room for two nights.

→ I'm planning to go to Paris for eight days and need to book a flight.

→ Do you have a table for four for this coming Saturday?

Taking Reservations

→ When are you looking / planning to fly?

→ What day / time / time frame are you considering / thinking of?

→ How many nights are you planning to stay?

Asking Questions About Prices and Rates

→ Do you have any special rates or discounts?

→ How much is the fare / the daily rate?

(☐ See page 71 for more phrases.)

Changes and Cancellations

Appointments and reservations, just like your busy life, are subject to events that have a way of upsetting your plans and schedules.

Changing an Appointment, Booking, or Reservation

→ I'd like to change my appointment with Helen from 3:00 to 4:00, if that's possible.

→ Could you move my appointment to next week?

→ I'm sorry, but I won't be able to make it to my appointment with James. Could you give me another time?

→ I need to change my reservation for tomorrow.

Canceling an Appointment, Booking, or Reservation

→ I'm sorry, but I'm afraid I have to cancel / postpone / call off my 3:00 appointment.

→ Unfortunately I won't be able to make it to my appointment with Einar.

→ Sorry, but I can't keep my dental appointment.

Orders and Services

Nowadays many products and services are available online. Nevertheless, you may choose to place orders more directly and personally over the telephone.

Ordering Food

Ordering from a restaurant that offers takeout service is fairly uncomplicated. For additional convenience, you can even find a good selection of menus in the phone book, and unless you prefer to pick up your order, most places deliver for a small fee, or for free if you place an order that exceeds the minimum. If you live in an apartment, you may need to give your buzzer code to the person taking the order so the delivery person can enter the building.

→ **I'd like to order** a large pizza supreme for delivery.

→ **Could I have / get** a family-size order of fried chicken for pickup?

Asking About Details

→ Do you deliver?

→ Is there a minimum order for delivery?

→ How much do you charge for delivery / extra salami?

→ How long will it take to get here?

→ What time can I expect delivery?

➜ What are your daily specials?

➜ Which dishes are gluten-free / lactose-free / vegetarian / vegan?

Taking an Order for Food

➜ Will that be pickup or delivery?

➜ Would you like any side dishes / extra sauces / beverages to go with your order?

➜ What time would you like that to be ready?

➜ We'll have that ready in about twenty minutes.

Ordering Products and Services

➜ I'd like to order a product / to reserve tickets / to cancel a subscription.

➜ Could I put in an order for a product / reserve seats on a flight?

➜ Would it be possible to open / set up / apply for an account ?

Arranging Utility Services

➜ I'd like to have my phone / cable / Internet hooked up / suspended / disconnected.

➜ Would you see that my phone / cable / Internet is hooked up as of the first of the month?

➜ I need telephone / cable service at my new address.

Arranging Transportation

→ Could you send a taxi to 54 River Road?

→ I need a taxi / a shuttle to the airport tomorrow morning at 6:30.

→ I'm registered at your hotel and need a ride / a pickup.

→ Please have a taxi pick me up at the Four Seasons Hotel.

Discussing a Problem

When discussing a problem on the phone, it's important to provide background information:

- your account number, if you have one
- the model and serial number, if you're having problems with a particular machine
- how you first contacted the company or person
- the last time you spoke or were in contact

Stating the Problem

→ **I was wondering if** you could explain the charges on my bank statement.

→ **It appears that** my subscription to your magazine has been renewed by mistake.

→ **I have a question about** this month's credit card statement.

→ **There's a problem with** my Internet service.

→ **We've been having some issues with** our copy machines.

→ **Can't you do something about** the ongoing noise?

Drawing Attention to a Problem

If you're not getting a helpful response to a complaint, you might need to use stronger language to make the person you're dealing with pay attention.

→ **Here's the thing**: the shipping delay is holding up production.

→ **It's like this**: we need the parts urgently.

→ **Listen here**: this is just not acceptable.

→ **Wait a minute**, that's not what I said.

→ **Now**, I have an important question.

Asking for Assistance

→ **How do I go about** renewing / suspending / canceling my cable subscription?

→ **Could you explain how** I can apply for a credit card?

→ **You wouldn't happen to know** where / how I can take out a membership?

Reporting an Urgent Problem

→ I need to report a stolen credit card / an accident / a break-in.

→ Can someone help me right away?

→ This is an emergency!

Dealing with a Problem

→ What seems to be the problem / trouble?

→ What can I do to help?

→ How can I assist / help you?

Showing Understanding and Sympathy

→ I understand where you're coming from.

→ I see the problem / issue.

→ I know what you mean.

→ That's unfortunate / too bad.

(☐ See page 96 for more phrases.)

Promising Action

→ I'll see that's taken care of as soon as possible.

→ I'll get on that / follow up on that right away.

→ Don't worry, I'll deal with it.

→ I'll do my best.

→ I'm on it!

Encouraging Further Contact

→ We look forward to doing business with you again.

→ Don't hesitate to call / reach out if you need anything else.

→ We're happy to be of service.

→ Call anytime.

In Conclusion

Because the content of a telephone conversation does not differ greatly from a regular face-to-face conversation, you can use many of the phrases in Parts 1 and 2. Particularly helpful phrases are:

- Staying in Touch, page 13.
- Making Offers, page 51.
- Advice and Assistance, page 97.
- Complaints, page 105.
- Options and Alternatives, page 119.
- Reasons and Purpose, page 120.
- Advantages and Disadvantages, page 122.
- Setting Schedules and Deadlines, page 130.
- Goals and Plans, page 131.
- Solutions and Recommendations, page 164.
- Clarification and Explanations, page 183.
- Misunderstandings, page 185.

Dialogue: Making an Appointment

A: Good afternoon. Community Clinic. Renée speaking. How can I help you?

B: Hello, this is Will Jameson. I'm calling to make an appointment to see Dr. Winter. It's about a checkup.

A: All right, what day would you like to come in?

B: Tuesday or Wednesday would be good, and I'd prefer late afternoon if you have an opening.

A: Let me see. Wednesday's pretty full. How does 3:30 on Tuesday suit you?

B: Yes, 3:30 works for me.

A: All right, I'll put you down. And the name was?

B: Will Jameson.

A: And it was for a checkup, you said?

B: That's right.

A: Okay then, Will. We'll see you on Tuesday at 3:30.

B: Thanks a lot!

A: No problem. Is there anything else I can help you with?

B: No, thanks. That'll be it. Good-bye now.

A: Good-bye.

Topics for Practice

What phrases would you use to:

1. book a flight to New York;
2. order a subscription to a local newspaper;
3. cancel a hotel reservation;
4. check your availability for a meeting;
5. make an appointment for a haircut;
6. call for a taxi;
7. confirm an appointment;
8. suggest an alternative time for an appointment;
9. ask about a car rental agency's weekly rate;
10. change your appointment to next week?

Vocabulary Notes

_____

_____

_____

_____

_____

_____

_____

_____

_____

_____

_____

_____

_____

_____

_____

_____

_____

_____

_____

_____

CHAPTER 14

Telephone/Video Conferencing

Objectives

- to arrange a group telephone/video conference
- to lead and take part in a group telephone/video conference

❦

Thanks to communication technology, we no longer need to be physically present to discuss business with colleagues and associates or to stay in touch with family and friends. The usefulness of platforms such as Zoom, Skype, Facetime, Teams, and Hangouts has been most evident during the COVID-19 pandemic. With more people staying and working at home, these teleconferencing tools have become the next best thing to being there.

While Facetime and Hangouts with friends and family is more fun, spontaneous, and even a little chaotic, doing business on Zoom with people from different countries requires not only careful preparation and organization, but also a command of specific phrases. After all, everyone wants to contribute, and everyone wants to be understood.

(i) As in the rest of the book, the phrases in this chapter are listed from formal to informal.

Phrases

Preparing the Call

The first step in arranging a tele/video conference, of course, is getting participants together. Invitations or notifications to join can be given on a formal or informal basis, depending on how well participants know each other, how often they've taken part, and the nature of the discussion.

A productive tele/video conference depends on preparation, and participants will need to know what is expected of them.

Inviting and Notifying Participants

→ I was wondering **if you can / are able / would like to take part in / attend** a conference call?

→ **I'd like to invite you to** attend a conference call.

→ **I'll send you an invite for** (date and time).

→ **Are you available on** (date and time) for a Zoom call?

→ **Do you have time to** Skype on (date and time)?

Asking for Confirmation

→ **I'd appreciate it if** you'd confirm your attendance in an e-mail.

→ **Can you send me** a confirmation e-mail by (date)?

→ **I need you to confirm** by text or e-mail by (date)?

→ **Please accept** the meeting invite at your earliest convenience.

→ **Did you receive** my calendar invite?

→ **Just send me** a quick text or e-mail.

Etiquette and Protocol

Setting ground rules makes for a respectful and co-operative exchange as well as ensures that participants are not wasting their time.

Do:

- Be prepared and on time.
- Make sure your cell phone is turned off and there's no background noise.
- Identify yourself with your name whenever you speak.
- Put your microphone on mute when you're not speaking.

- Stick to the topic.
- Speak slowly and clearly when conversing with nonnative speakers.

Don't:

- Interrupt another speaker.
- Monopolize the conversation.

Introducing Protocol

→ Firstly / First off, I'd like to outline the rules / to set protocol.

→ I'd like to make everyone aware of today's rules / protocol.

→ Let's go over some rules first.

Limits and Restrictions

→ I ask you to make your comments short, relevant, and to the point.

→ I've allowed / allotted 10 minutes for discussion.

→ Would you please stick to the time limit.

→ Please keep your comments brief and to the point.

→ Please submit your comments by Chat.

→ Try not to stray from the topic / get sidetracked.

Taking Turns

→ Everyone will take turns / be given a chance to speak.

→ You are asked to stick to the agenda / stay on track.

➔ If you're not talking, please put yourself on mute.

➔ Please don't everyone talk at once.

➔ Please state your name and position first when it's your turn to speak.

➔ Use the "raise your hand" indicator to speak.

Getting Started

There are two roles in a tele/video conference: the **leader** or **chairperson**, and the **participants**. While the leader is responsible for running things smoothly, as well as seeing that everyone has his or her say, it is up to every participant to contribute according to protocol.

(See Greetings, page 21.)

Welcome

➔ My name is Silvia, and I'll be leading / conducting today's call.

➔ First off, I'd like to welcome everyone to today's call.

➔ Welcome to today's conference / meeting / session!

➔ Welcome, I hope everyone is doing well today.

➔ Thanks for joining in / taking part / participating!

➔ Thank you all for making the time to be here today.

➔ Nice to see all of you!

➔ Glad everyone could be here!

Introductions

→ To start, I'll have everyone introduce themselves.

→ Let's introduce ourselves, starting with Rafael.

→ How about saying your name and a little bit about yourself?

→ Please say your name and role at [organization].

(See Introducing Yourself, page 9, and Making Introductions, page 24.)

Small Talk

If the number of participants and time permit, a little small talk can serve as **a warm-up**.

Some common topics are:

→ the weather	How's the weather on your end? / I hear you've had a lot of rain lately.
→ well-being	How've you been? / How are things? / I hope you're all well.
→ catching up	It's been awhile since we last talked. / Long time since we talked.
→ personal achievement	I hear you just got married. / Congratulations on your promotion!
→ family	How is your son doing? / Did you visit your sister for the holidays?

Checking Attendance

➜ Is everyone ready/ connected / online?

➜ I think we are still waiting for Juanita to join.

➜ Can we go ahead / proceed now?

➜ Are we missing anyone?

➜ Shall we give Monica two more minutes to attend?

➜ Let's start with a roll call.

> (i) A **roll call** involves someone calling out a list of names to check attendance.

Responses

➜ I'm here / present.

➜ Yes, that's me!

➜ Here!

➜ Present!

Absentees

➜ I regret / am afraid Bernhardt won't be attending / joining.

➜ We'll have to proceed without Vikram who will be absent today.

➜ Nadia has asked me to excuse her.

➜ Kanista's sorry she can't be here but sends her regards.

➜ Jonathan is unable to join as he's on vacation.

Starters

→ If everyone's ready, we can begin.

→ Let's begin / get started / kick this off / get the ball rolling!

→ Can we start now?

→ I'm going to be recording the meeting.

→ So, here goes! / Here we go.

(See additional phrases, page [173].)

Preliminary Business

Once everyone has introduced themselves and knows the **procedure**, participants need to be informed of the **agenda**.

Outlining the Agenda

→ Does everyone have a copy of the agenda?

→ Has everyone received / looked over the agenda?

→ As you'll see, there are three items on today's agenda.

Last Minutes

→ I'll quickly / briefly go over the minutes of our last conference.

→ Let's take a moment to review the minutes of the last meeting.

ⓘ The **minutes** of a meeting have nothing to do with time; rather, they refer to the notes that were recorded during the last conference.

Stating Objectives

→ The **purpose / aim / objective** of our meeting **is to** touch base.

→ Today **we want / plan / hope to review** our latest sales figures.

→ I've called this meeting / conference **to discuss** the new price list.

→ I've called you together **to discuss / evaluate / report on** online sales.

→ This will be a recurring meeting **to monitor** our advertising spend.

Recent Developments

→ **Let's go over** the most recent developments since our last meeting.

→ Muriel, can you **get / bring us up to speed on** last quarter's balance sheet.

→ Jose will **give us an update** / will **bring us up to date on** new hiring guidelines.

→ **How is** the renovation **progressing** / **coming along** / **moving forward**?

→ **What's the status of** / **the latest on** our payroll upgrade?

→ **Where do we stand on** net-zero emission targets?

Referring to Documents

→ Does everyone have a copy of the document / report?

→ If you'll look at / take a look at / turn to page [3].

→ Please let me know if you can't see my shared screen.

→ I'll share my screen.

→ Turn to page 6.

→ The point is in bold / highlighted.

→ I'll add a link to the document in the Chat.

Discussion

In terms of content and language, tele/video conferences don't differ from any other business meeting or discussion.

Asking for Feedback

→ I'd like to hear what Idris has to say / to offer.

→ Alex, can you step in here / give us your take / say a few words?

→ Feel free to offer / give us your input / jump in with your feedback.

→ Does anyone have something to add?

→ Guido, would you like to comment?

→ Let's hear from Sina!

→ Let me read out some of the comments on Chat.

→ Can you add your two cents?

(i) You are best advised to use the expression **to add or give your two cents** only with people you know very well, as it can sound like you don't value the person's input very much.

Finishing the Topic

➜ That takes care of / wraps up / covers that point!

➜ If there's nothing more / further to add, we can move on to the next item.

➜ That's all for now on that point!

➜ Now, let's move / go on / turn to the next point!

➜ Can you please share the next slide / slideshow on your screen?

Additional phrases are found in Part 2, Chapters 7–9:

Problems

When it works, technology is wonderful. When it doesn't, it can be a pain in the neck!

Audio Problems

→ I'm afraid you're cutting out / fading out / breaking up.

→ We can see you but there's no audio.

→ There's some interference / background noise.

→ Please turn up the volume / sound.

→ Can everyone hear me all right?

→ Does anyone have a problem with the volume?

→ We need to check everyone's microphone.

→ Simone, I think you cut out for a moment.

→ Could everyone put themselves on mute, please?

→ Sonia, I think you're on mute.

→ John, unmute yourself!

Video Problems

→ I can't see your shared screen.

→ We can hear you, but we can't see you.

→ Your picture is frozen / jerky / breaking up.

→ Can you repeat that, please? It looked like you were frozen.

→ Sorry, the screen shows only a poor Internet connection.

Language Problems

➔ I'm sorry, but I don't understand.

➔ Do you think you could repeat that / say that again?

➔ I didn't get that. Could you please repeat?

➔ What do you mean?

➔ What are you trying to say?

➔ Please speak more slowly / more clearly.

Additional phrases are listed on:

■ Clarification and Explanations, pages 183–185.

■ Misunderstandings, pages 185–188.

Taking Action

Making decisions and taking action can be the most challenging, but most necessary, part of a tele/video conference.

Delegating Responsibility

➔ I was wondering if you would take responsibility for / take charge of the next meeting.

➔ I'll leave this in your capable hands.

➔ Would you take care of / look after / follow up on this?

➔ I'll hand this task over to you.

➔ I'll leave that up to you.

➔ That's your field of expertise.

■ Setting a Deadline

→ **The deadline is** the end of the month.

→ **I'd like to have this done by** Thursday / the 15th / the end of the month.

→ **This should be ready by** Tuesday at the latest.

Additional phrases are listed on:

- ■ Options and Alternatives, pages 119–120.
- ■ Advantage and Disadvantages, pages 122–123.
- ■ Making a Decision, pages 124–128.
- ■ Setting Schedules and Deadlines, pages 130–131.
- ■ Suggestions, pages 97–99.
- ■ Solutions and Recommendations, pages 164–165.

■ Summarizing

To make sure that everyone leaves the discussion **on the same page**, it will be necessary to conclude the conference with a summary of the main points or decisions.

→ To sum up / re-cap, ...

→ Let me summarize ...

→ Could I have your final comments?

(See additional phrases, page 191.)

Follow-Up

➔ When can we do this / get together again?

➔ Any suggestions for a follow-up call?

➔ When can we meet again?

➔ Let's schedule another meeting in [time].

Ending the Call

➔ It's time to finish up / to wrap things up / to conclude our discussion / close the call.

➔ It looks like we're running out / we've run out of time.

➔ We're almost at time.

➔ We're approaching the hour.

➔ We have a hard stop at [time].

➔ I realize we have run out of time, but could you please stay for a few more minutes?

➔ Let's bring things to a close.

➔ That about does it for today.

➔ That's it for today / this time.

➔ You can all hang up now.

➔ Time's up!

Dialogue: Let's Get the Ball Rolling!

The following dialogue gives you an idea of how a tele-video conference might begin. Underline or highlight the phrases from the chapter.

Jenn: Good morning, everybody! First, I want to thank both of you for taking the time for this call today!

Dave: Hi, Jenn. It's good to see you!

Jenn: Same here. Dave, you know Tara, don't you? She's joining us from San Francisco.

Dave: Ya, hi, Tara. How've you been?

Tara: Not too bad under the circumstances.

Dave: Unfortunately, this pandemic has really messed things up.

Jenn: It sure has! But at least we can touch base on Zoom!

Dave: Thank goodness for that!

Tara: You can say that again!

Jenn: By the way, Mark won't be joining us and sends his regards.

Tara: That's too bad. He always has lots of good ideas.

Jenn: Maybe next time. Anyway, as you know, the reason I got you together is to touch base and see how the new website is coming along. I trust you got my e-mail with the results of our customer survey?

Tara: I did.

Dave: In fact, I've got it here in front of me.

Jenn: Great! Then let's get the ball rolling! I think you both know the protocol!

Dave: Sure do! My cell phone's off.

Tara: Sorry, Jenn. but your video's frozen.

Jenn: Can you hear me?

Tara: I can but I can't see you.

Dave: It must be a poor Internet connection.

Tara: Wait, now you're back.

Jenn: Good! OK then. Dave, I'll start with your progress report but Tara, feel free to jump in with your feedback.

Topics for Practice

What phrases would you use to:

1. delegate responsibility;
2. interrupt the speaker;
3. ask someone to turn off his/her cell phone;
4. start the video call;
5. let the participants know that you can't hear them;
6. welcome participants to the call;
7. state the purpose of the call;
8. ask for feedback;
9. set the rules;
10. end the call?

Vocabulary Notes

_____

_____

_____

_____

_____

_____

_____

_____

_____

_____

_____

_____

_____

_____

_____

_____

_____

_____

_____

_____

_____

About the Author

Diane Engelhardt holds bachelor degrees in Education (Secondary) and English Literature (Honors). She began teaching English as a Second Language at Berlitz School of Languages in Nuremberg, Germany. Over her long career, she taught conversational, business and academic English in Germany and Canada, and conducted TESL courses for prospective ESL teachers. Her other publications with McGraw Hill Educational are: *Practice Makes Perfect Intermediate English Reading and Comprehension, Practice Makes Perfect Advanced English Reading and Comprehension,* and *Essential Vocabulary for the TOEFL Test.*

Index

This index help you find the most common phrases, grouped by theme, from Chapters 1–10.